TANKS OF WORLD WAR II UP CLOSE

MILITARY TECHNOLOGY: TOP SECRET CLEARANCE

TANKS OF WORLD WAR II UP CLOSE

MARTIN J. DOUGHERTY

ROSEN PUBLISHING
New York

ILLUSTRATIONS BY COLIN PEARSON

This edition published in 2016 by:
The Rosen Publishing Group, Inc.
29 East 21st Street
New York, NY 10010

Library of Congress Cataloging-in-Publication Data

Dougherty, Martin J.
Tanks of World War II up close / Martin J. Dougherty.
Includes index.
ISBN 978-1-5081-7086-0 (library bound)
World War, 1939-1945--Tank warfare--Juvenile literature. | Tanks (Military science)--History--Juvenile literature.
UG446.5 D68 2016
623.7'4752'09044--dc23

Manufactured in the United States of America

Contents

Introduction

The term 'Armoured Fighting Vehicle' (AFV) is both a title and a description of what an AFV is and what it does. A successful AFV must balance three elements within its design – firepower, protection and mobility. This is a complex tradeoff, and it is not possible to build a single vehicle that can do everything to a world-beating degree. On the other hand, a design that involves too many compromises may end up being outclassed by its competitors as it tries to be all things to all men.

Before the outbreak of World War II, AFVs were generally considered to be a support system for the infantry rather than a decisive arm in their own right. They were intended to help infantry get across contested terrain and into the enemy positions, eliminating strongpoints as they went. Thus early tanks were intended to fight against infantry and perhaps artillery positions, but not other tanks.

T-26

A 'Breakthrough Weapon'

Although some notable thinkers pushed for an aggressive armoured combat doctrine in the inter-war years, this did not immediately come about. Most nations retained the idea of the tank as a short-ranged 'breakthrough' weapon to be used in carefully prepared offensives against defended positions.

Even in Germany there was doubt as to exactly what could be expected of the armoured forces, as well as a reluctance to allow the hard-charging Panzer generals to undertake the sort of reckless, deep-penetration and exploitation offensives for which they were arguing. Indeed, there is a common misconception that the German invasion of Poland in 1939 was a *Blitzkrieg;* in fact, the armoured troops were used cautiously and in support of a general advance rather than leading it.

It was only when the German armoured forces essentially ran out of control during

Sherman

the invasion of France that their capabilities were truly demonstrated. This was a huge gamble, staking hopes of victory on an untried doctrine that used weapons which nobody was entirely sure could deliver the results promised by their proponents. In the event, the rapid fall of France proved the pro-Panzer lobby correct.

World War II Developments

World War II created an environment of extremely rapid development and innovation, with vast rewards for the nations that made the right predictions about what weapon systems would be needed in a year's time and how they were best to be used. From this crucible emerged the principles of armoured warfare and the sort of vehicles needed for them.

First and foremost, tanks needed to be able to fight other tanks. The best response to an armoured assault was a counter-attack with mobile armoured forces, sealing off any breach in the defensive line and possibly making a breakthrough after defeating and pursuing the enemy armoured force. In order to defeat other armoured vehicles, a tank needed a gun capable of penetrating their armour, coupled with a good sighting system and sufficient armour protection to ensure that the tank could survive the encounter.

Mobility was also vital, both on the offensive and the defensive. Short-range cross-country performance had to be combined with sufficient speed and range to redeploy to meet an attack or to punch through the enemy line and exploit the breakthrough. This also allowed deep 'pincer' attacks, cutting off large enemy forces in a 'cauldron' where they could be finished off by infantry, artillery and air attack.

It was in these fast-moving offensives that armoured forces demonstrated how much warfare had changed between 1916 and 1940. In World War I, offensives rarely reached the enemy rear echelon and thus rarely achieved more than local success. An armoured breakthrough allowed fast-moving forces to rampage through the enemy rear, destroying support formations, disrupting the logistics chain and overrunning headquarters to throw enemy forces into disarray. This meant the whole strategic situation could now be altered with a single bold stroke.

KV-85

Tank Types

Three general types of tank emerged during the war. Light tanks were primarily useful for reconnaissance, flank security and exploitation of a breakthrough.

MARDER III

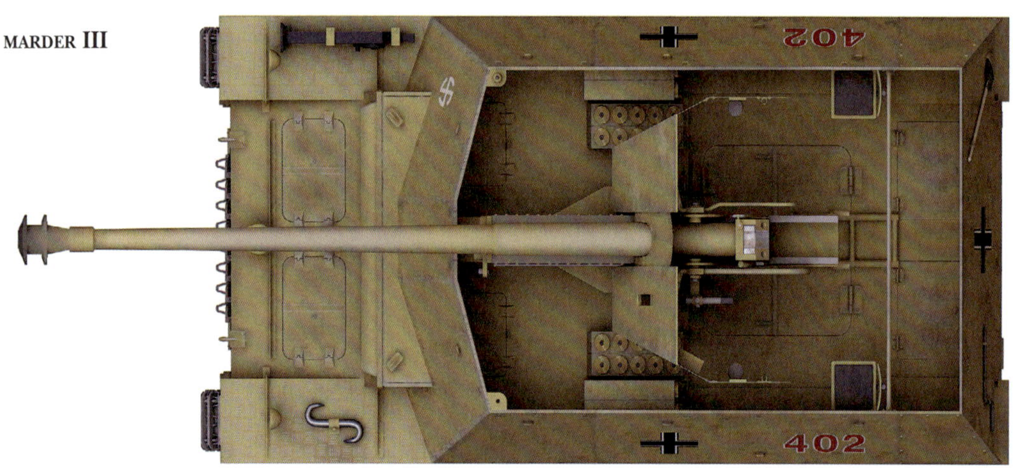

However, because they were cheap, light tanks were built in huge numbers between the wars and were often pushed into roles for which they were too lightly protected.

Medium tanks were workhorse designs with good protection and armament, capable of undertaking most tasks. In many cases, medium tank designs were divided between those intended for infantry support (often called Infantry Tanks) and those intended for wide-ranging operations (Cruiser Tanks). Over time a more general-purpose medium tank emerged, with one design capable of undertaking a variety of roles. This was the beginning of the modern Main Battle Tank concept.

Heavy tanks were generally considered useful for breaking through heavy enemy defences or repulsing an armoured assault. Their low speed and limited range meant that they were rarely capable of great strategic mobility or fast-moving exploitation, but they could make the initial breakthrough, which could then be followed up by lighter vehicles.

KETTENKRAFTRAD

Mobile Armoured Infantry Carriers

With the tank emerging as the primary offensive instrument, it became obvious that rather than limiting tank forces to the speed of the infantry and artillery, more could be achieved by creating highly mobile armoured infantry carriers, logistics vehicles and self-propelled artillery that could keep up with the armoured formations.

The earliest self-propelled guns were improvised affairs, but soon the vast numbers of obsolete tank chassis available to the combatants made it possible to use them for a variety of specialist vehicles, including air defence mounts and artillery tractors. One of the most useful conversions, which was pioneered by the German army, was the assault gun. This was essentially an artillery piece carried on an armoured chassis, making it capable of close-range support work.

A similar vehicle with an anti-tank gun could be effective on the defensive against tanks. In many cases, improvements in artillery technology allowed the assault gun and tank destroyer roles to be combined. These vehicles could get tank-calibre guns into action more cheaply than true tanks, but they were less versatile and could suffer severe losses if caught without adequate infantry or tank support. Despite this, they were often pushed into roles for which they were not suited, simply because they were available at the time. Later in the war, assault guns were commonly used as a substitute for tanks in German armoured formations.

Armoured vehicles capable of carrying infantry and supplies were often created by converting existing (usually obsolete) tank chassis, but in some cases were custom designed. Even the German army, which had embraced mechanization earlier than any other force, relied heavily on foot and horse transport at the start of the war. However, by its end most armed forces were heavily mechanized, a trend that continues to this day.

Creating the Digital Models

Every vehicle in this book was originally created as a complex 3D object, using computer graphics software commonly employed in the production of movies and video games. From the 3D model, each of the seven-view images was generated, or rendered, from various viewpoints of the model (above, below, and so on). The result is a set of highly detailed 2D images suitable for printing.

1 All 3D objects start with a single point, called a vertex. Its position in the virtual 'space' in the graphics program can be defined by three parameters: X, Y and Z or, in more basic terms, left and right, up and down, and back and forth.

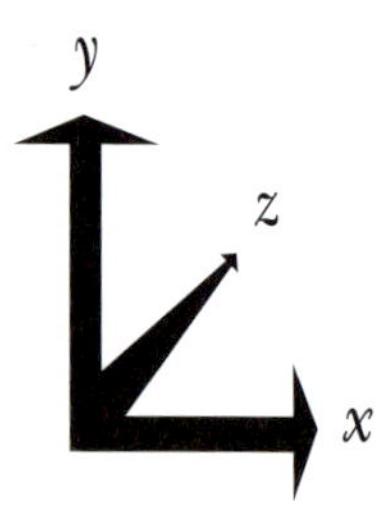

2 Once you have three vertices, they can be joined to form a 2D triangle in 3D space, called an edged face.

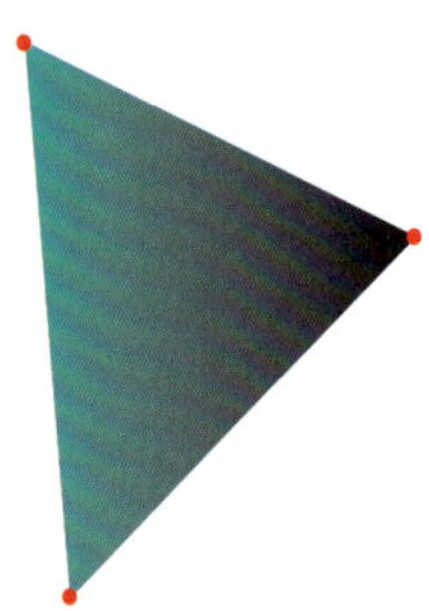

3 To begin creating a gun, for example, the computer graphics program 'lathes' hundreds of 2D shapes in the Z axis, drawing a barrel shape in three dimensions around the X axis. Every point is defined by different values for X and Y.

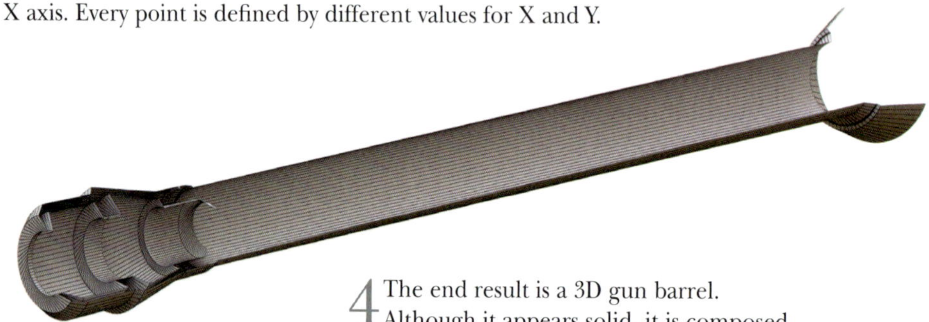

4 The end result is a 3D gun barrel. Although it appears solid, it is composed of hundreds of edged faces, themselves made up of lines and vertices.

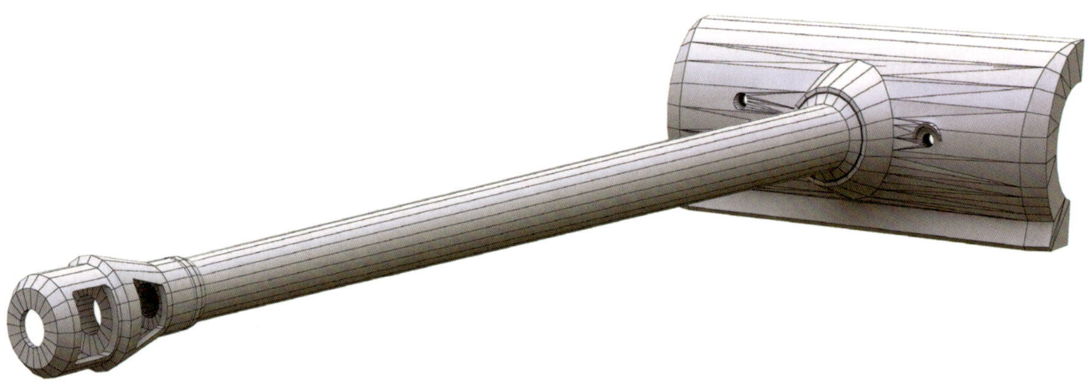

5 To create more complex objects, simple elements are fitted together to form an assembly like this gun from the Panther tank.

6 A texture is applied to the finished gun, to give the appearance of painted steel (see below). Texture is applied by wrapping a stored 2D texture around a 3D object. The finished 3D gun can be textured, painted and lit. Finally it can be rendered from any angle.

7 The finished tank models on the following pages are all constructed of many hundreds and thousands of individual edged faces, rendered and textured from different angles. This is a German Panther tank.

Whippet

The Medium Mark A Tank, better known as the Whippet, was conceived as a 'cavalry tank' – i.e. a fairly light tank that would cooperate with cavalry in order to make a breakthrough of the enemy line. This could then be exploited by cavalry in the traditional manner. The Whippet was the first tank that could be driven by a single operator, using separate engines to drive each track. It could travel at twice the speed of a MkI tank on level ground, though this was still not enough to keep up with advancing cavalry. However, experience in the field proved that once the cavalry met resistance they would be stalled while the tanks were able to continue their stately advance. Whippet tanks proved their worth in the field almost immediately. In one of their first actions, a depleted company of seven Whippets punched through the enemy lines in line-abreast formation, and then in the best traditions of the cavalry they were designed to work with, smashed back through the enemy formations to return to their own lines.

- Light, fast tank with a crew of three
- Machine gun armament mounted on the sides of a fixed superstructure
- Poorly ventilated and very hot inside the crew compartment

SPECIFICATIONS

Country of Origin: *United Kingdom*

Crew: *3 or 4*

Weight: *14,300kg (31,460lb)*

Dimensions: *Length 6.10m (20ft); width 2.62m (8ft 7in); height 2.74m (9ft)*

Range: *257km (160 miles)*

Armour: *5–14mm (0.2–0.55in)*

Armament: *Four Hotchkiss machine guns*

Powerplant: *Two 33.6kW (45hp) Tylor four-cylinder petrol engines*

Performance: *Maximum road speed 13.4km/h (8.3mph)*

9
A249
IX

9
A249
XI

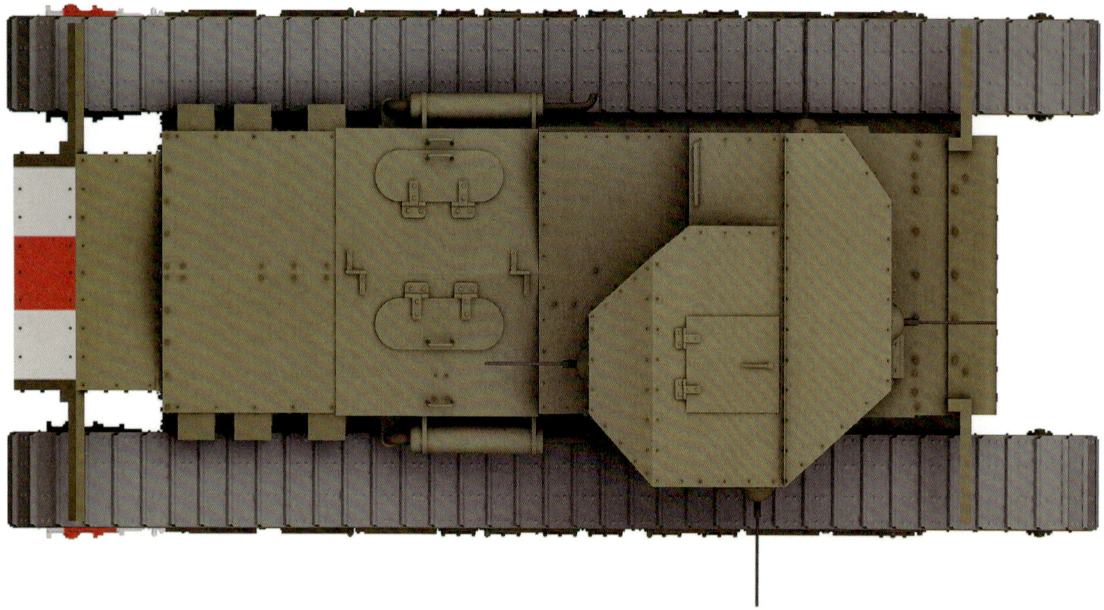

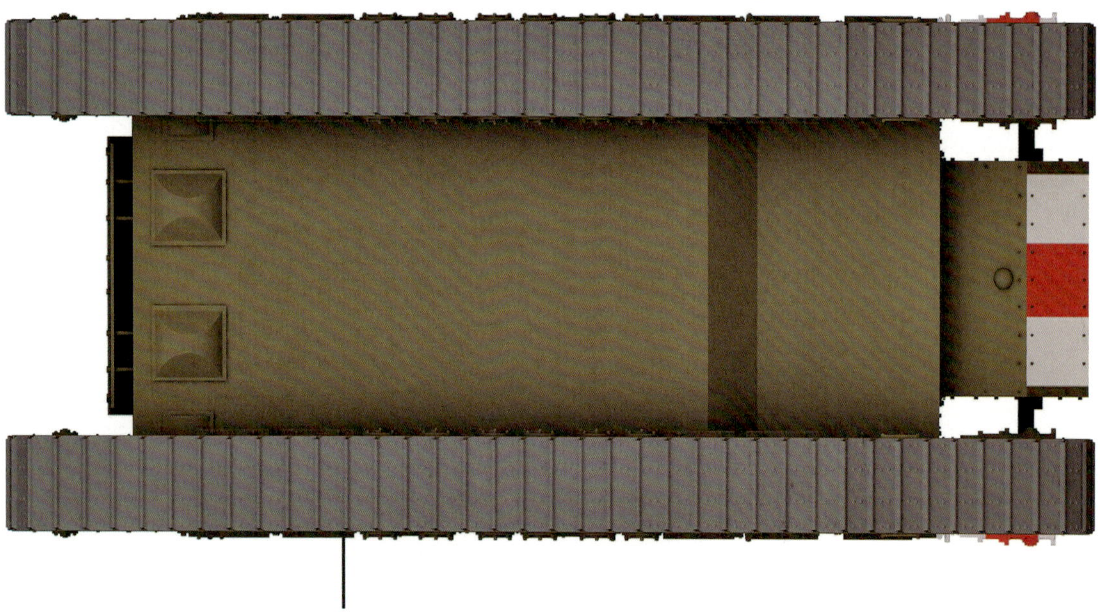

Whippet
A Whippet tank named 'Musical Box' made the world's first armoured exploitation in August 1918. Cut off after breaking through the enemy lines, the tank crew embarked on a nine-hour rampage through the enemy's rear area before finally being disabled by artillery.

UNUSUAL FEATURES

The Whippet mounted its engine in the front of the vehicle, an unusual feature in tank design. The fuel tank was originally in the rear but was moved forward before mass production began. Other changes were made during the design process. The original intent was to mount a rotating turret, but this was replaced by an armoured pillbox-like structure housing four machine guns to give all-round fire capability.

The Whippet's crew of three was remarkably small for the time, though an extra gunner was sometimes carried. Another unusual feature was the concentration of the crew in a single compartment. Up to that point, tanks had large crews dispersed over a fairly large vehicle, making communications and coordination difficult in action. The Whippet thus represented a move towards far more efficient armoured vehicles.

Renault FT-17

The FT-17 was developed as an infantry support vehicle. For this role it needed to be little faster than a walking man, though trench-crossing capability was important. Construction was extremely simple; rather than build the tank on a chassis, the hull itself served as the chassis. The FT-17 was proof against small arms fire, which was considered sufficient for its envisaged role. Not only was speed extremely limited, but the FT-17 carried only enough fuel for about 35km (21.7 miles). This was adequate for its projected role as a mobile gun or machine gun emplacement intended to assist an infantry advance, but limited the tank's capacity for later development. The FT-17 mounted its weapons in a rotating turret atop the hull, the first tank to do so. The initial armament was an 8mm (0.3in) machine gun, which was soon followed by a version carrying a short 37mm (1.45in) gun. Several other versions were constructed, including a turretless command tank and small numbers armed with a 75mm (2.95in) gun. Experimental models were built to carry searchlights and to clear mines, and as a radio vehicle.

- Small infantry support tank with a crew of two
- Very slow and short-ranged
- First tank with a rotating turret

SPECIFICATIONS

Country of Origin: *France*

Crew: *2*

Weight: *6600kg (14,520lb)*

Dimensions: *Length with tail 5m (16ft 5in); width 1.71m (5ft 7.33in); height 2.133m (7ft)*

Range: *35.4km (22 miles)*

Armour: *16mm (0.63in)*

Armament: *One 37mm (1.45in) gun or one machine gun*

Powerplant: *One 26kW (35hp) Renault four-cylinder petrol engine*

Performance: *Maximum road speed 7.7km/h (4.8mph)*

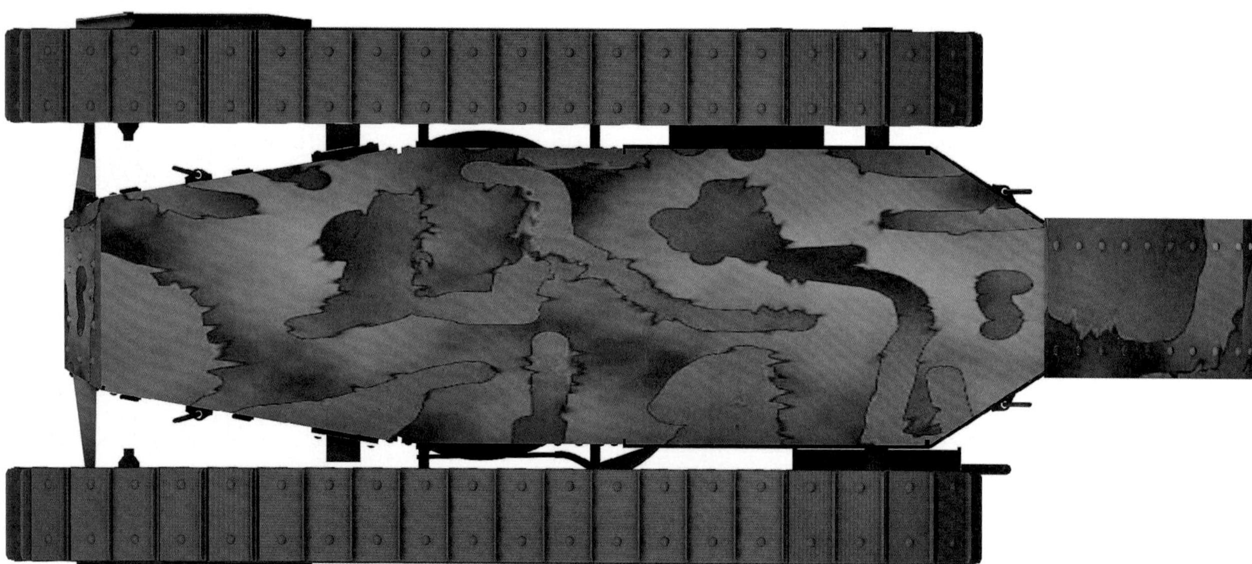

Renault FT-17

The distinctive 'tail' on the back of the FT-17's hull was designed to assist in trench-crossing. Its designed role was to attack deeply-entrenched troops across shell-cratered ground.

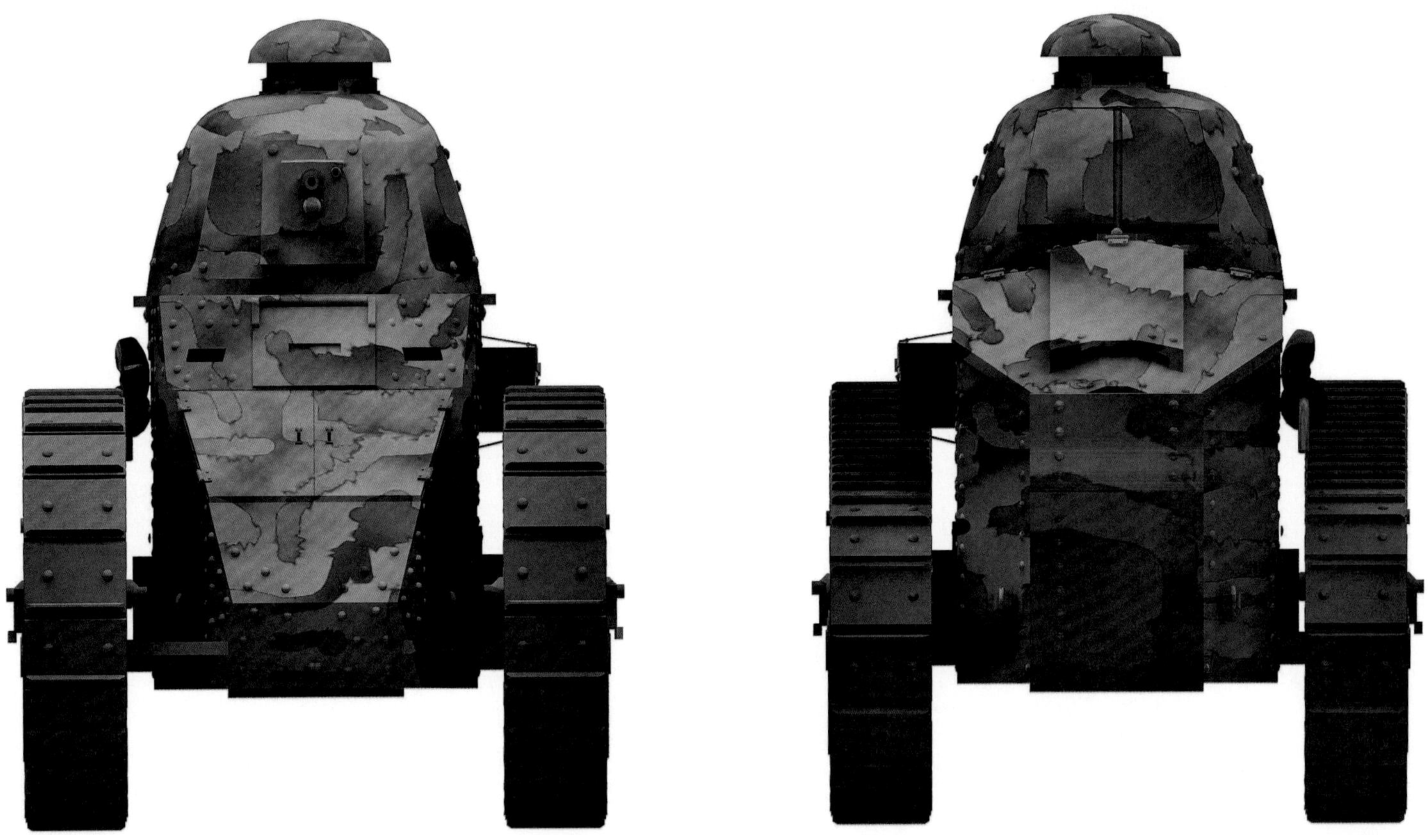

MASS PRODUCTION

Huge numbers of FT-17s were built, with the first entering combat in May 1918. Four thousand were ordered in France alone, and copies were built in other countries. This was a mixed blessing; with so many vehicles available and facing difficult economic conditions, France did not feel the need to spend a lot of money on tank development and production after the end of the war. These 'legacy' vehicles soldiered on through the 1920s and even the 1930s, and although new tanks were produced, about 1300 FT-17s were still in French service at the outbreak of World War II. They were hopelessly inadequate and played no useful part in the Battle of France. Many fell into German hands and were pressed into service for occupation duties or converted to other roles such as artillery tractors.

T-26

The T-26 was based on the British Vickers 6-ton light tank. It was designed for infantry support and was pushed into production as the T-26A before it had been properly evaluated. At the time of its introduction, multi-turret tanks were popular, and the T-26A went into service with twin turrets normally each carrying a gunner and a single 7.62mm (0.3in) machine gun. The left-hand turret also contained the vehicle commander. Some T-26As carried a .50 calibre (12.7mm) heavy machine gun in one turret and a 7.62mm machine gun in the other, while those designated as 'artillery tanks' replaced one machine gun with a 27mm (1in) or 37mm (1.45in) gun. However, experience showed that twin turrets were ineffective, and the T-26B was developed with a more conventional single, large, turret. The T-26B initially mounted a 37mm (1.45in) gun, but this was later upgraded to a 45mm (1.8in) gun. Riveted construction was replaced by welding as a result of experiences in Manchuria. It was noted that rivet heads could pop off and endanger the crew as secondary projectiles even when the armour was not penetrated by enemy fire.

- Light tank, with a crew of four (later three)
- Initially equipped with two turrets and two gunners
- Later versions were conventional designs

SPECIFICATIONS

Country of Origin: *Soviet Union*

Crew: *3*

Weight: *10,400kg (22,932lb)*

Dimensions: *Length 4.8m (15ft 8in); width 2.39 (7ft 10in); height 2.33m (7ft 8in)*

Range: *200km (125 miles)*

Armour: *6–15mm (0.2–0.6in)*

Armament: *One 37mm (1.45in) gun Model 28; one 7.62mm (0.3in) machine gun*

Powerplant: *One GAZ T-26 eight-cylinder petrol engine developing 68kW (91hp)*

Performance: *Maximum road speed 28km/h (17mph)*

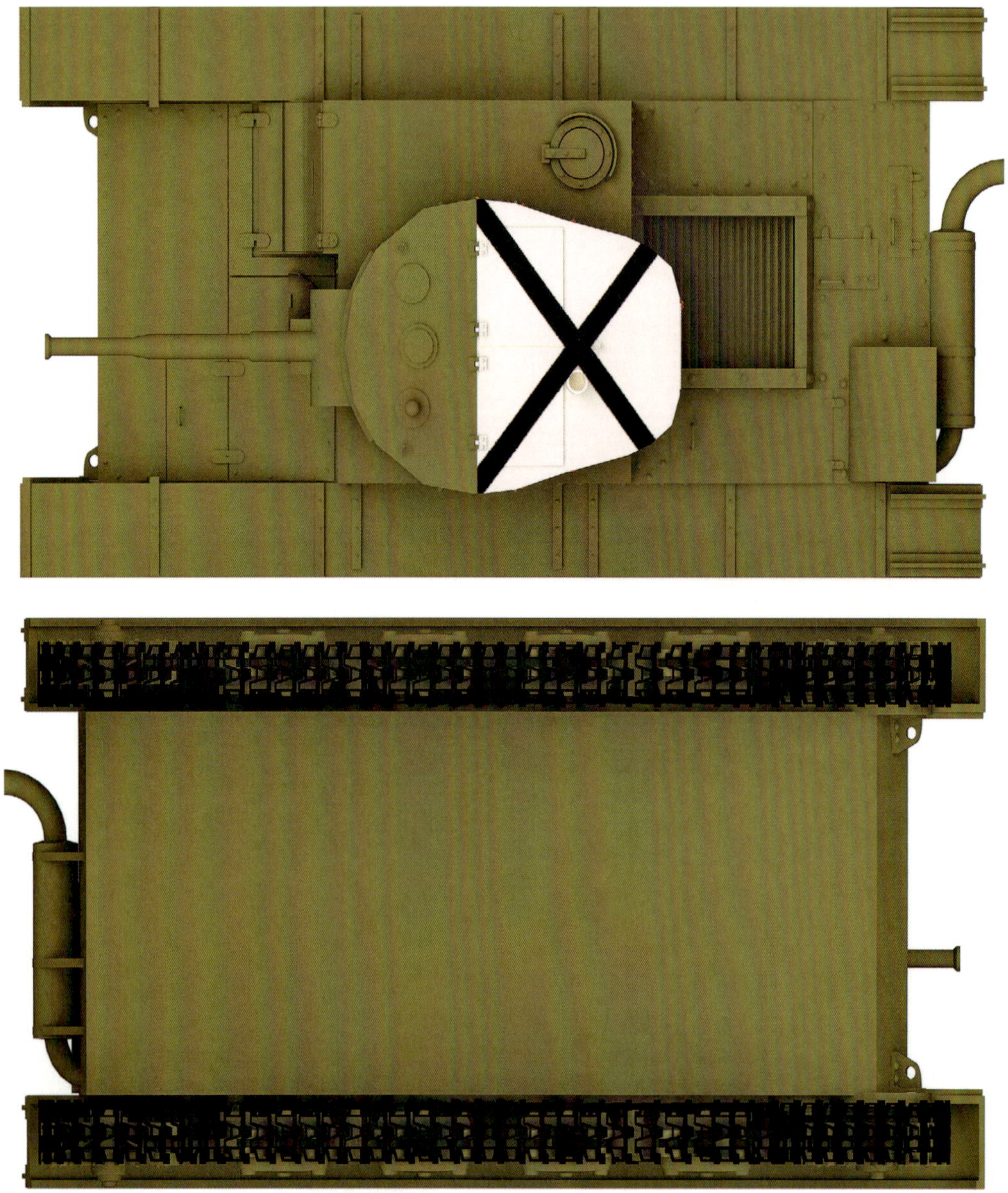

T-26

The T-26 was gradually improved as a result of combat experience. Conical turrets, intended to deflect enemy fire, were introduced after the Spanish Civil War, and welded construction was used after experience in Manchuria demonstrated the hazards of riveting tank hulls.

HUGE LOSSES

Robust and reliable, and greatly improved over the original version, the T-26 gave good service in clashes with Japan in the 1930s, but this was largely due to the fact that Japan's tanks were also inadequate. The T-26 belonged to an earlier era of tank design and was outdated by the time that World War II broke out. However, it was available in vast numbers and was thrown into the fighting, where it suffered immense losses against the more advanced and better armed tanks of the German Army. Those vehicles that survived were withdrawn from front-line service. As with other obsolete tanks, it was used as the basis for experimental vehicles, including self-propelled artillery, bridgelayers and (without success) a glider tank. The T-26's main contribution to the Soviet war effort was in establishing mass-production practices and allowing experience of large-scale armoured operations to be gained.

PzKpfw I

The Panzerkampfwagen (Armoured Fighting Vehicle) Mk I was never intended to be a front-line battle tank. It was constructed as a training vehicle for Germany's rapidly expanding armoured forces, and to enable experience to be gained. Nevertheless, it was available in large numbers at the outbreak of World War II and had to serve until better-armed vehicles were available in sufficient numbers. The first model (Ausf A) was built as a mass prototype. Many vehicles had no turrets and were used for driver training. The Ausf B was slightly longer and became the standard PzKpfw I chassis, with over 6000 built. The PzKpfw I Ausf B was equipped with a small turret mounting two 7.92mm (0.31in) machine guns. This vehicle was entirely suitable for use as a light infantry-support tank or reconnaissance vehicle, but was not ideal for the role that it was forced to undertake as backbone of the armoured forces. The PzKpfw I was withdrawn from front-line service as soon as more capable vehicles became available, and its chassis was used for a series of experimental variants and conversions.

- Light tank with a crew of two
- Armament of two general-purpose machine guns
- Used as the basis for many specialist vehicles

SPECIFICATIONS

Country of Origin: *Germany*

Crew: *2*

Weight: *5500kg (12,100lb)*

Dimensions: *Length 4.02m (13ft 2in); width 2.06m (6ft 7in); height 1.72m (5ft 7in)*

Range: *145km (81 miles)*

Armour: *6–13mm (0.2–0.5in)*

Armament: *Two 7.92mm (0.31in) MG13 machine guns*

Powerplant: *One Krupp M305 petrol engine developing 45kW (60hp)*

Performance: *Maximum road speed 37km/h (21mph); fording 0.85m (2ft 10in); vertical obstacle 0.42m (1ft 5in); trench 1.75m (5ft 9in)*

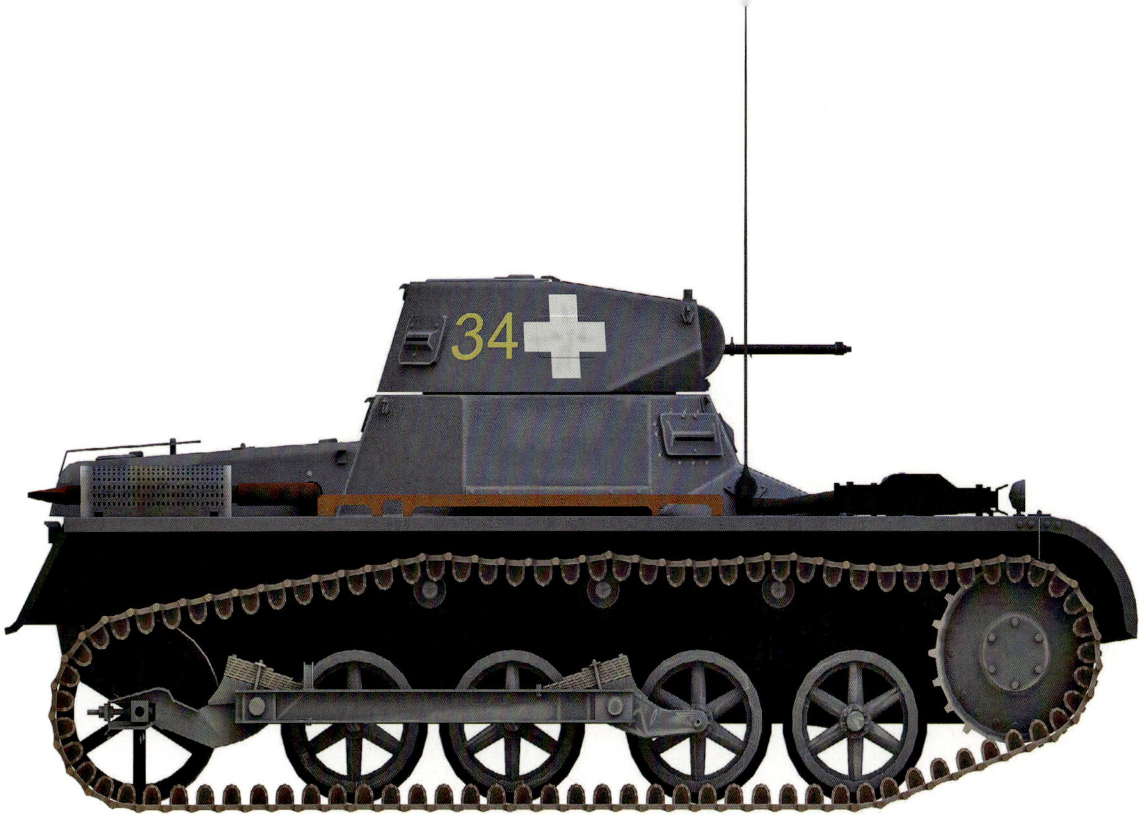
34

34

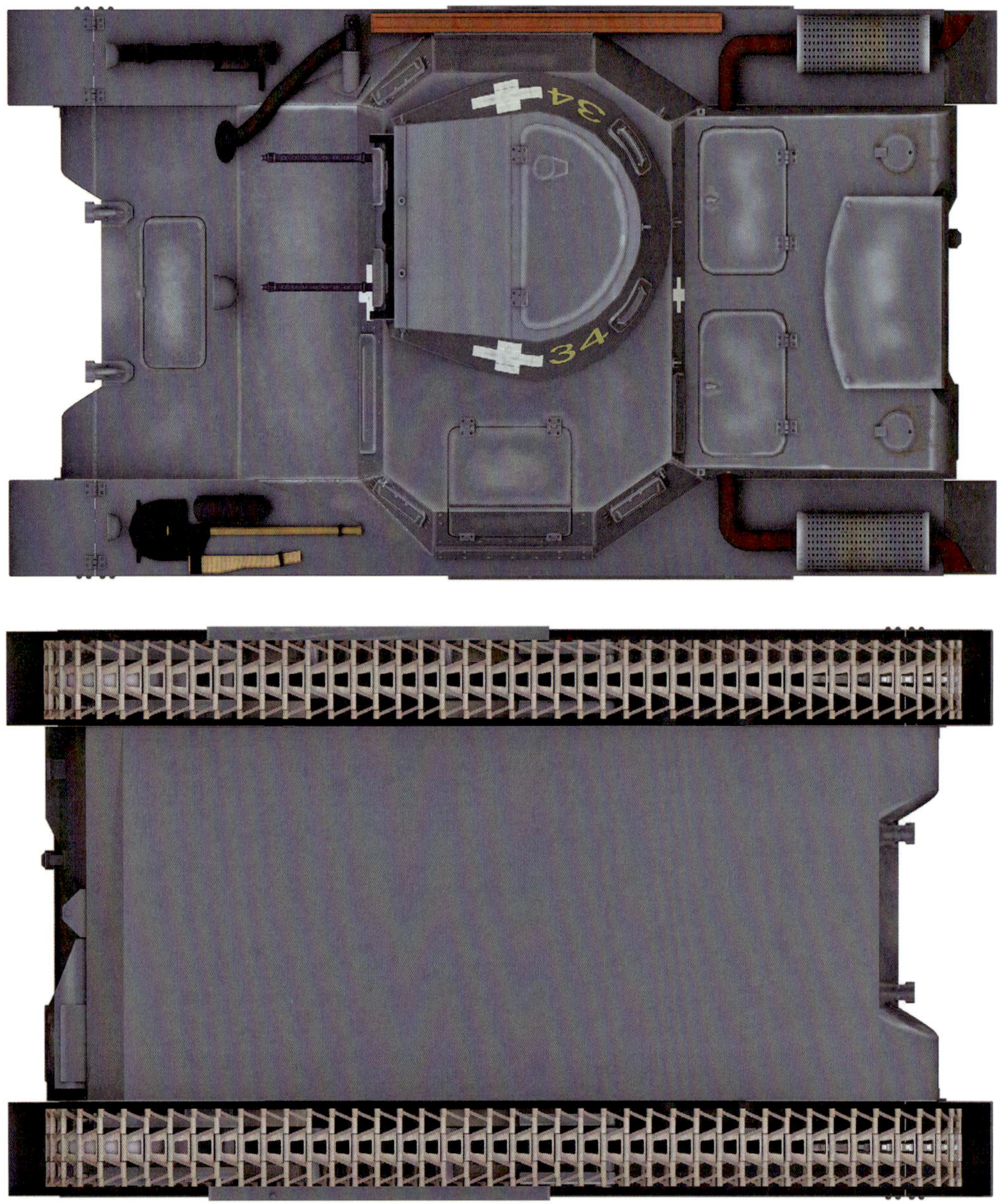
34
34

PzKpfw I

The PzKpfw I made its combat debut in the Spanish Civil War, in an arena where anti-tank threats were few and the most likely target was enemy infantry. When it met enemy tanks, the Panzer 1 was often outmatched.

GOOD RESULTS

Although inadequate in many ways, the PzKpfw I formed a large part of an aggressively handled armoured force which achieved impressive results in Poland and France. It was fast and protected against small arms fire, and therefore entirely capable of overcoming enemy positions that would hold up unsupported infantry. This was the tank's original role, and the PzKpfw I was a very useful vehicle in areas where there were few anti-tank weapons or enemy tanks. However, there was nothing that a Panzer I could do against armoured vehicles, even ones as poorly armoured as itself, and its protection was inadequate to protect it against even light anti-tank weapons. It could not fight tanks, and it was obvious that this capability was of paramount importance. It was replaced in front-line service as quickly as better vehicles became available.

133
133

PzKpfw II

Experience in the Spanish Civil War showed that Pzkpfw Is could disable Soviet-supplied T-26 light tanks at short range using armour-piercing ammunition in their machine guns, but were powerless at longer ranges. Requests for a version armed with a 20mm (0.79in) gun resulted in a handful of prototypes, which may have influenced the development of the Pzkpfw II. After a series of experimental models, the Pzkpfw II went into service armed with a 20mm (0.79in) gun and a co-axial 7.92mm (0.31in) machine gun. This was sufficient to deal with light tanks of the time and for anti-personnel work, but the tank's armour was very light. This was rectified after the Pzkpfw II saw action in 1939–40, but there was a limit to what the chassis could carry. Variants and upgraded versions continued to appear as the war went on, including a dedicated reconnaissance tank built in small numbers in 1943–44. By this time the Panzer II was badly outmatched on the battlefield and was steadily withdrawn. Many were converted for other roles, including self-propelled guns, supply carriers, artillery tractors and tank destroyers mounting 50mm (1.97in) or 75mm (2.95in) guns.

- Light tank with a crew of three
- Armour was initially proof only against small arms and shell fragments
- Served as the basis of many specialist vehicles

SPECIFICATIONS

Country of Origin: *Germany*

Crew: *3*

Weight: *10,000kg (22,046lb)*

Dimensions: *Length 4.64m (15ft 3in); width 2.30m (7ft 6.5in); height 2.02m (6ft 7.5in)*

Range: *200km (125 miles)*

Armour (Ausf F version): *20–35mm (0.8–1.38in)*

Armament: *One 20mm (0.79in) cannon; one 7.92mm (0.31in) machine gun*

Powerplant: *One Maybach six-cylinder petrol engine developing 104kW (140hp)*

Performance: *Maximum road speed 55km/h (34mph); fording 0.85m (2ft 10in); vertical obstacle 0.42m (1ft 5in); trench 1.75m (5ft 9in)*

R

R

R
R

PzKpfw II

After construction of PzKpfw II tanks ceased, production of chassis continued as the basis for the Wespe 105mm (4.1in) self-propelled howitzer and flamethrowing tanks. Experimental tanks were also constructed on the PzKpfw II chassis, including a bridgelayer and an amphibious version. The latter was originally conceived for the invasion of Britain, but eventually served on the Eastern Front.

LIMITATIONS

Built on the same chassis as the Panzer I, the PzKpfw II was limited by its size and small turret ring. Its 20mm (0.79in) gun was sufficient to disable light armoured vehicles but was inadequate against medium tanks. Protection was still scanty, and experience in 1939–40 prompted the addition of more armour. This came at the price of reduced speed and agility, which are arguably the main assets of the light tank. It became clear that little more could be achieved with the PzKpfw II as a combat tank and it was phased out, though later in the war a developed version designated PzKpfw II Ausf L Luchs was produced. Created specifically as a light armoured reconnaissance tank, this was what the Panzer II should always have been, but few were built.

Type 97 Chi-Ha

The Type 97 was little more than an enlarged version of the Type 95 light tank. The chassis was significantly longer, with six roadwheels rather than the four of the Type 95, and it had a two-man turret. However, compared to Allied medium tanks the Type 97 was vastly under-armoured. It was primarily intended for infantry support, dealing with machine gun positions, rather than to fight other tanks and for this role it was adequate. However, against troops equipped to fight European tank forces, the Type 97 fared very badly. Initial armament was a 57mm (2.24in) gun and two machine guns, but from 1942 onwards a new variant became available, named Shinhoto (which simply meant 'modified turret'). This mounted a high-velocity 47mm (1.85in) gun, with improved anti-armour performance. The Shinhoto variant was produced for the rest of the war and became the main tank of the Japanese armed forces. Japanese tank production was never undertaken on a huge scale because the navy absorbed most of Japan's heavy industrial production, notably in terms of steelmaking.

- Medium tank with a crew of four
- Very lightly protected
- Main Japanese tank during World War II

SPECIFICATIONS

Country of Origin: *Japan*

Crew: *4*

Weight: *15,000kg (33,069lb)*

Dimensions: *Length 5.5m (18ft); width 2.33m (7ft 8in); height 2.23m (7ft 4in)*

Range: *240km (149 miles)*

Armour: *Not available*

Armament: *One 57mm (2.24in) gun type 97; two 7.7mm (0.303in) Type 99 MG*

Powerplant: *One Mitsubishi Type 97 V-12 diesel engine developing 127kW (170hp)*

Performance: *Maximum road speed 39km/h (24mph)*

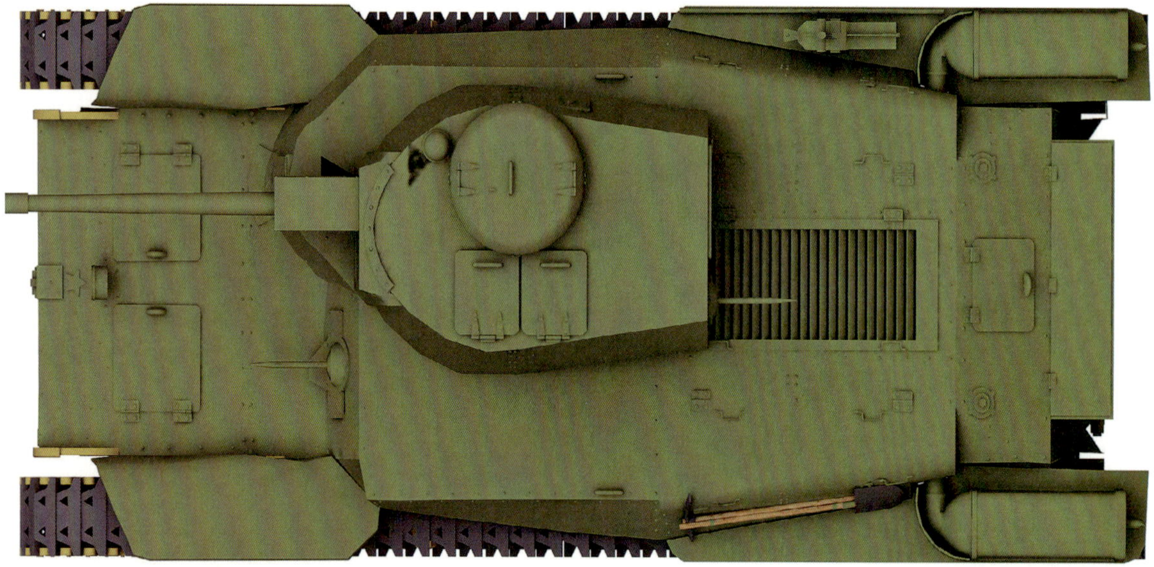

Type 97 Chi-Ha
The Type 97 originally carried a low-velocity 57mm (2.24in) gun in its offset turret. This weapon was adequate for engaging machine gun positions with high explosive shells but was not up to the task of dealing with enemy tanks. A high-velocity 47mm (1.85in) gun was fitted as a result of wartime experience.

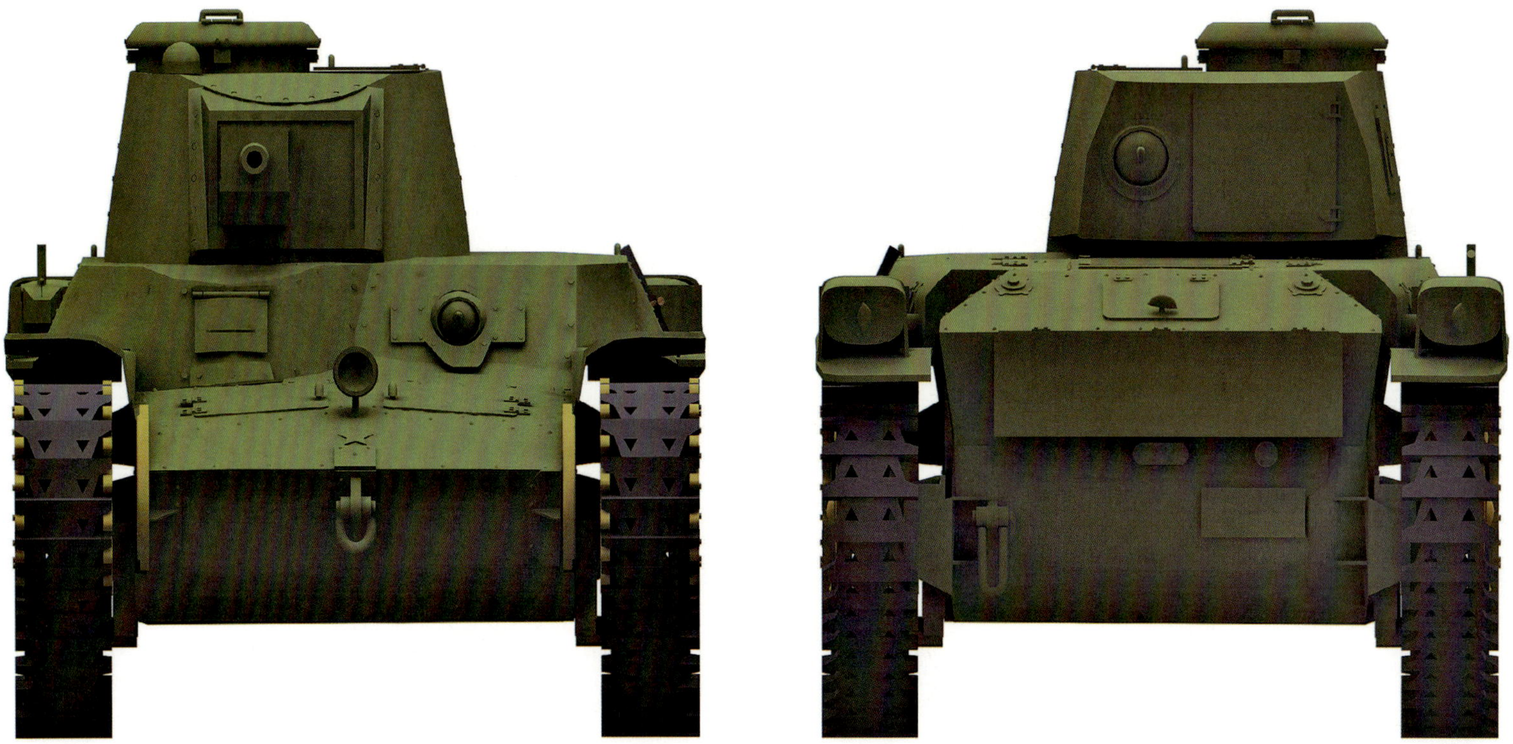

HARD WORK

Japanese expectations of what sort of tanks the army would require were coloured by their experiences in Manchuria, where the ill-equipped and disorganized Chinese were overcome with relative ease. Light tanks and even tankettes were found to be perfectly adequate to take on regional militias with few anti-tank weapons. The decision to build a 'medium' tank with extremely light protection makes sense in this context, especially since naval production took the lion's share of Japanese steel output. Building thinly-armoured vehicles did at least mean that sufficient numbers could be produced. However, the Type 97 was inadequate in other ways. Its turret was hand-cranked, a significant disadvantage in highly mobile combat where turret traverse speed might mean the difference between victory and defeat. The gun was also manually elevated by the gunner, which was both imprecise and extremely tiring.

M3 Stuart

As involvement in European war became increasingly likely, the United States perceived a need to upgrade its tank forces. With no time to develop a new tank, the decision was taken to improve the M2 Light Tank. The new vehicle's designation, M3, risked confusion with the M3 medium tank, so the names of Civil War generals began to be assigned to tank designs. The M3 thus became the Stuart. The M3 was given thicker and better constructed armour than its predecessor, and a new cast turret to reduce weight. This contained the world's first gyro-stabilized main gun and also mounted remotely operated machine guns. The suspension was also improved, reducing ground pressure and improving cross-country performance. The M3 was a fast, agile and mechanically reliable vehicle, well-liked by its crews. Its gyro-stabilized gun allowed accurate firing on the move, a capability no other tank at that time possessed. However, the M3 was behind the times as an overall design. By the time it entered service, such vehicles were no longer viable as front-line combat units, except in the Pacific theatre against inadequate Japanese armoured forces.

- Fast light tank with a crew of four
- Gyro-stabilized 37mm (1.45in) gun
- Reliable even under desert conditions

SPECIFICATIONS

Country of Origin: *USA*

Crew: *4*

Weight: *12,927kg (28,440lb)*

Dimensions: *Length 4.54m (14ft 10.75in); width 2.24m (7ft 4in); height 2.30m (7ft 6.5in)*

Range: *112.6km (70 miles)*

Armour: *15–43mm (0.59–1.69in)*

Armament: *One 37mm (1.45in) gun; two 7.7mm (0.303in) machine guns*

Powerplant: *One Continental W-970-9A six-cylinder radial petrol engine developing 186.5kW (250hp)*

Performance: *Maximum road speed 58km/h (36mph); fording 0.91m (3ft); vertical obstacle 0.61m (2ft); trench 1.83m (6ft)*

2
U.S.A. W - 303580 MC301

2
MC301 U.S.A. W - 303580

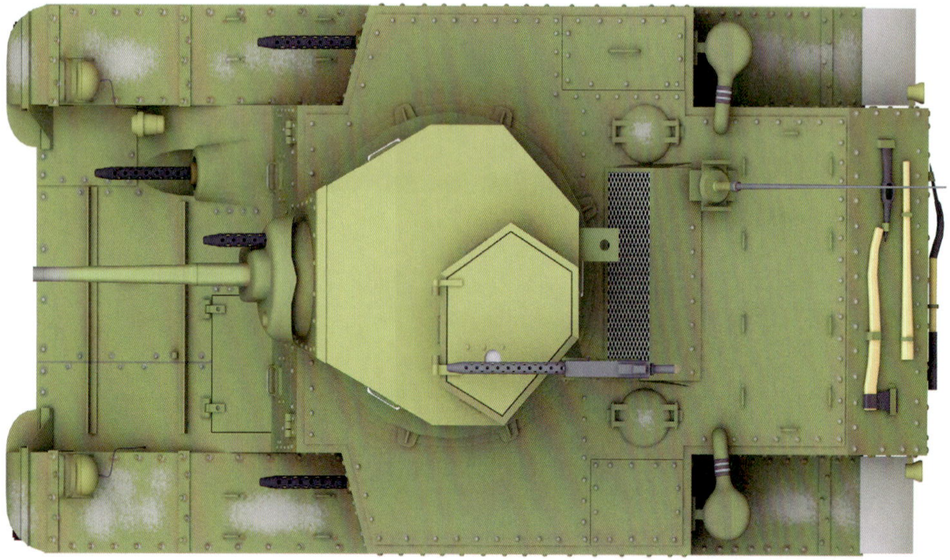

M3 Stuart

A number of changes were made to M3s that entered British service. The external machine guns were removed and their sponsons used for stowage. British crews liked the M3 so much that they called it 'a Honey', and the name stuck.

LIGHT TANKS

Tight economic conditions in the 1930s made light tanks attractive to many nations, which in turn led to a situation where most anti-tank weapons were designed to defeat lightly-armoured vehicles. Thus for a time, light tanks were adequate for the battle tank role, and they had the added advantage of being cheap enough to be produced quickly in the numbers required for a major war.

The move towards better-armoured medium and cruiser tanks, and the consequent development of weapons designed to defeat them, meant that light tanks like the M3 were no longer viable as front-line armoured combat vehicles. However, they were available in quantity and medium tanks were not, so the M3 had to do the best it could. It was retasked as a reconnaissance asset as soon as heavier tanks were available.

LAURA, HERE WE COME

BT-5

Early Soviet tank designs owed much to the work of the American designer J Walter Christie, and the first four designs in the BT series used the Christie engine. The BT-5, however, was given a newly developed powerplant derived from an aircraft engine. The BT series were designated cavalry tanks and were designed for speed and mobility. The BT-5 used the Christie suspension and was able to run on either tracks or road wheels, steering by turning the front wheels. Later designs using the same suspension, such as the T-34, did not have this capability, which faded away as a passing novelty. Although lightly armoured, the BT-5 was fast and armed with a 45mm (1.78in) gun. This was a heavy armament at the time, and the BT-5 was able to outrange and destroy the Panzer Is it encountered in the Spanish Civil War. BT-5s saw combat against Finnish forces in the Winter War, and were deployed in large numbers against the German invasion of 1941. However, by that time the BT-5 was outclassed and was easily destroyed by its opponents. Losses were high, and the surviving vehicles were soon replaced by the infinitely more capable T-34.

- Light tank with a crew of three
- 45mm (1.78in) gun represented heavy armament for the time
- Used the proven Christie suspension system

SPECIFICATIONS

Country of Origin: *Soviet Union*

Crew: *3*

Weight: *11,500kg (25,357lb)*

Dimensions: *Length 5.58m (18ft 3in); width 2.23m (7ft 3in); height 2.25m (7ft 5in)*

Range: *200km (124 miles)*

Armour: *6–13 mm (0.2–0.5in)*

Armament: *One 45mm (1.78in) model 1932 gun; one 7.62mm (0.3in) coaxial DT MG*

Powerplant: *One Model M-5 developing 298kW (400hp)*

Performance: *Maximum road speed 72km/h (44mph)*

725

725

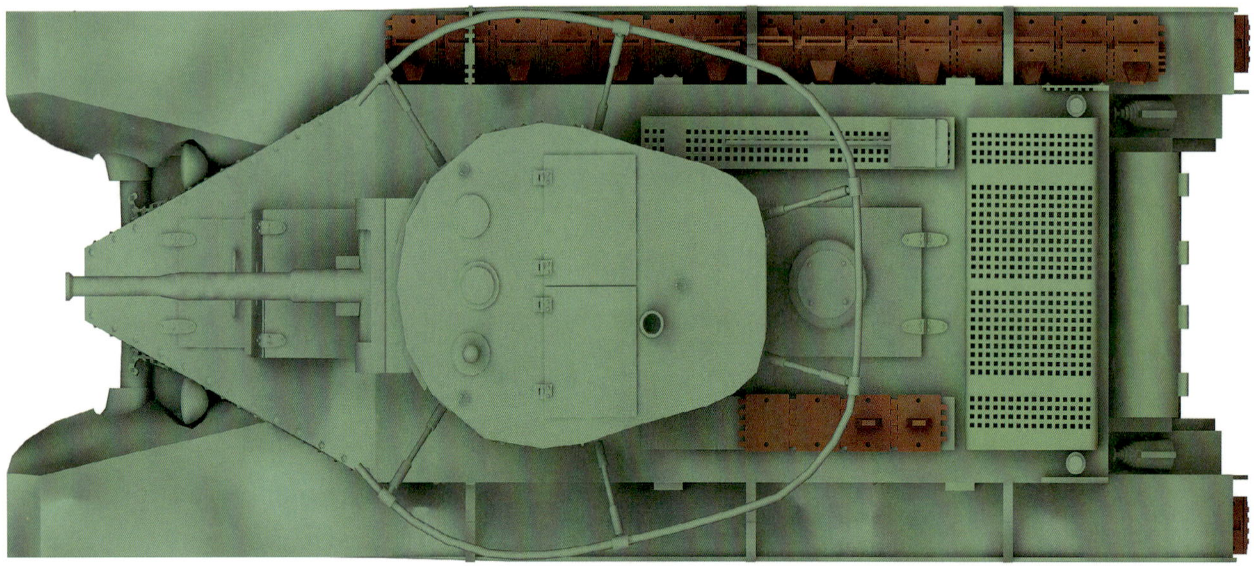

BT-5
During the Spanish Civil War it was discovered that the German Panzer I could penetrate a BT-5 at close range using armour-piercing ammunition from its machine guns, but was a helpless target at medium or long range.

BRITISH INFLUENCES

The BT-5 was the best tank of the interwar era, and in many ways foreshadowed modern tank design. At a time when designers were coming up with clumsy multi-turreted monstrosities or machine gun-armed vehicles that could not take on other tanks, the BT-5 was fast, tough and armed with a serious weapon. Its 45mm (1.78in) cannon outgunned most likely opponents, although it was still a light tank and not heavily armoured. The BT-5's superiority was demonstrated in Manchuria and the Spanish Civil War, but by the time the Soviet Union was invaded in 1941, it was becoming obsolescent. Nevertheless it embodied the key concepts of tank design – armour, mobility and a weapon powerful enough to be effective, in a balance suitable to the mission the tank is expected to carry out.

T-28

The T-28 was one of the first medium tank designs to go into mass production anywhere in the world. It was developed for the breakthrough role, and was heavily influenced by both British and German designs. Although slow, it had good obstacle-crossing capabilities. Many components were shared with the T-35 heavy tank, which it was designed to complement. The T-28 was equipped with multiple turrets. The main armament was carried in a main turret with all-round traverse. This was initially a 45mm (1.78in) gun, but production models were fitted with a 76mm (3in) weapon instead. Some T-28s mounted a machine gun in the rear of the turret. In addition, the tank had two auxiliary turrets, each with a traverse of 220°, mounted forward. These initially carried a 45mm (1.78in) gun and a machine gun; production models were fitted with two machine guns. Armour was thin and poorly designed, with large slablike surfaces that did nothing to deflect incoming shells. The T-28 was the Soviet Union's first indigenously produced medium tank, and the project served to be something of a learning experience.

- Medium tank with a crew of six
- Inefficient multi-turret design
- Thin armour and low speed increased vulnerability

SPECIFICATIONS

Country of Origin: *Soviet Union*

Crew: *6*

Weight: *28,509kg (62,720lb)*

Dimensions: *Length 7.44m (24ft 4.8in); width 2.81m (9ft 2.75in); height 2.82m (9ft 3in)*

Range: *220km (136.7 miles)*

Armour: *10–80mm (0.39–3.15in)*

Armament: *One 76.2mm (3in) gun; three 7.62mm (0.3in) machine guns*

Powerplant: *One M-17 V-12 petrol engine developing 373kW (500hp)*

Performance: *Maximum road speed 37km/h (23mph); fording not known; vertical obstacle 1.04m (3ft 5in); trench 2.90m (9ft 6in)*

4

4

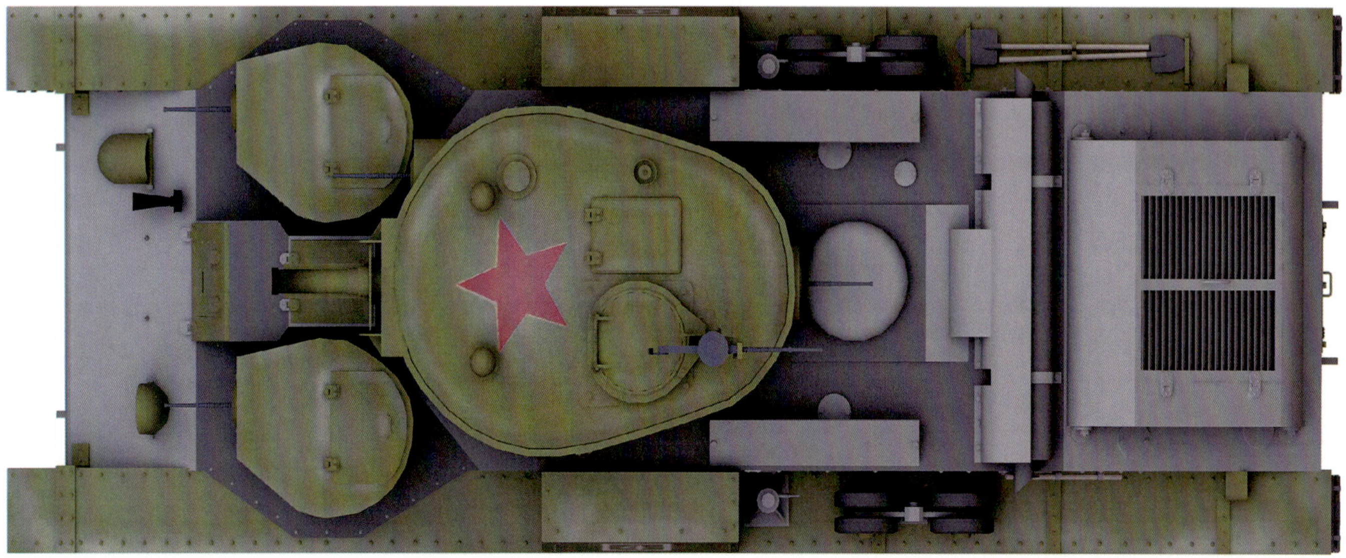

T-28
Although the Finnish army possessed little anti-armour capability, the T-28 proved easy prey for the few anti-tank guns they did have. Finnish gunners nicknamed the T-28 the 'Mail Train'.

A DIFFERENT WAR

The T-28 was clearly designed for the conditions encountered during World War I, with heavy frontal firepower and good obstacle-crossing capability. The nature of war had changed by the time it saw combat, and the T-28 was found lacking. In action in Finland its slow speed and weak armour resulted in heavy losses. An upgraded version with improved protection, designated T-28E, was fielded from 1940 onwards. However, the extra protection came in the form of appliqué armour, an inefficient upgrade that did little to counter the T-28's basic weaknesses. It was still a big, easy target with slab sides that were unlikely to deflect an armour-piercing round. Thrown into action to meet the German invasion in 1941, the T-28Es fared little better than other obsolete Soviet designs and suffered enormous losses.

Matilda

The Matilda Mark I was designed as an infantry tank. It was thus heavily armoured but armed only with a machine gun, and capable of similar speeds to infantry on foot. Budgetary concerns further constrained the designers. Designated A11, the Mk I Matilda proved to be reliable and supremely tough, but its lack of mobility and heavy armament forced an early retirement. Mating the reliability and survivability of the Mk I to a 2pdr (40mm/1.57in) gun capable of penetrating enemy tanks, the Mark II Matilda was available in small numbers at the outbreak of World War II. It proved virtually invulnerable to enemy anti-tank weapons, with only the 88mm (3.5in) gun capable of reliably penetrating its armour. However, even though the Mk II Matilda was significantly faster than its predecessor, it was too slow for the cruiser tank role forced on it during mobile operations in North Africa. There was also little room for improvement; the Matilda's turret ring was too small to allow a more powerful weapon to be mounted, so its offensive capability was left behind in the breakneck arms race of World War II. Mark II Matildas served throughout the war.

- Infantry-support tank with a crew of four
- Heavily armoured and reliable
- Too slow for tank warfare of the period

SPECIFICATIONS

Country of Origin: *United Kingdom*

Crew: *4*

Weight: *26,926kg (59,237lb)*

Dimensions: *Length 5.613m (18ft 5in); width 2.59m (8ft 6in); height 2.51m (8ft 3in)*

Range: *257km (160 miles)*

Armour: *20–78mm (0.8–3.1in)*

Armament: *One 2-pounder (40mm (1.57in) gun; one 7.92mm (0.31in) Besa machine gun*

Powerplant: *Two Leyland six-cylinder petrol engines each developing 71kW (95hp) or two AEC diesels each developing 65kW (87hp)*

Performance: *Maximum speed 24km/h (15mph); maximum cross-country speed 12.9km/h (8mph); fording 0.914m (3ft); vertical obstacle 0.609m (2ft); trench 2.133m (7ft)*

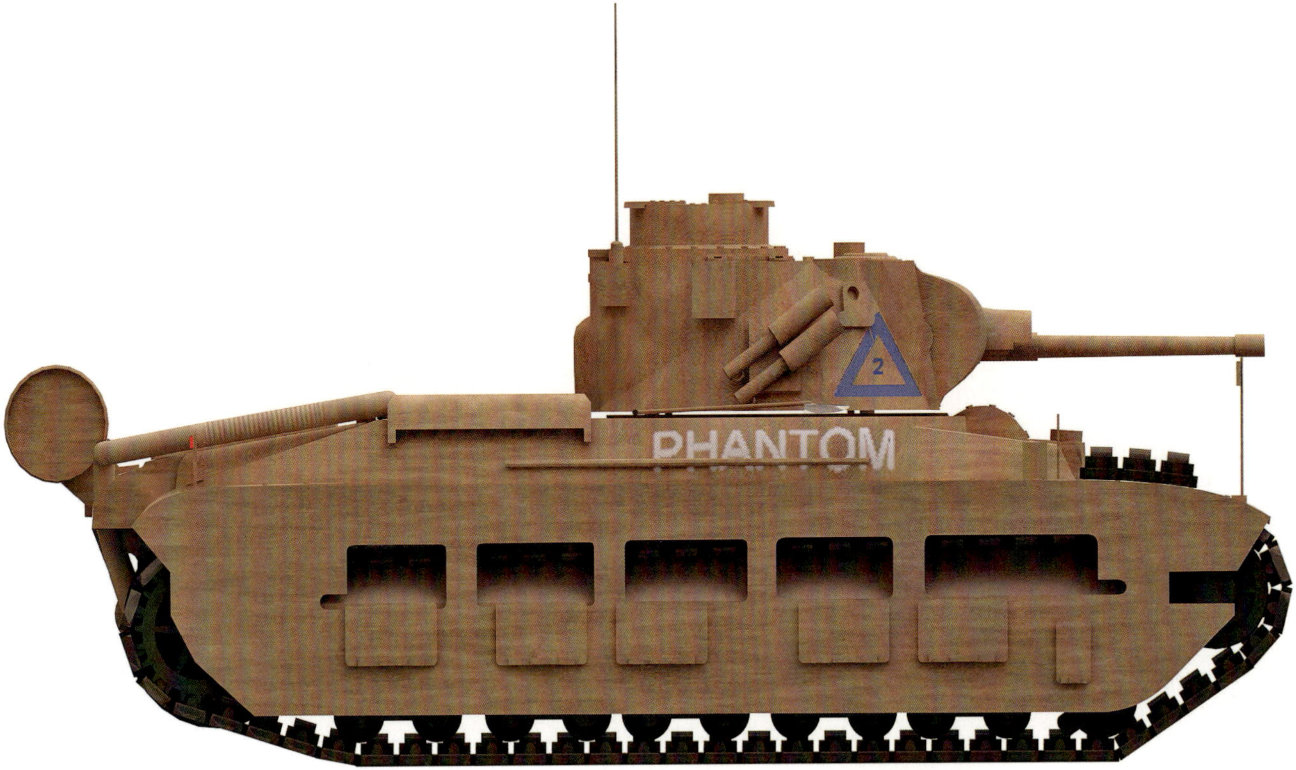
2
PHANTOM

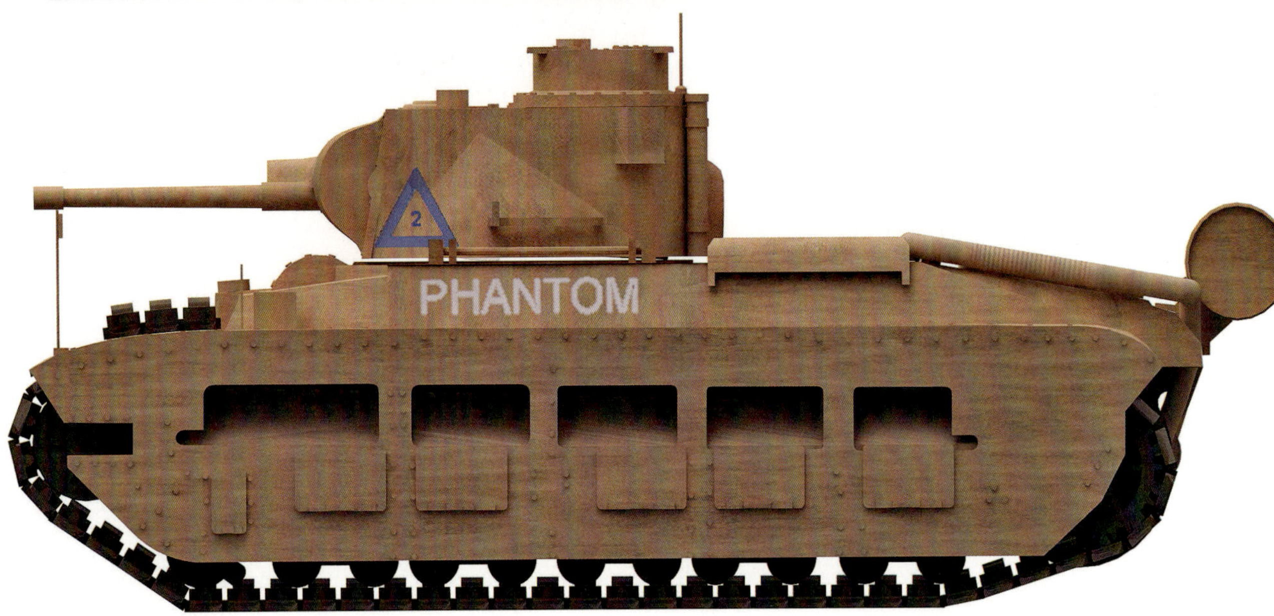
2
PHANTOM

PHANTOM
PHANTOM

52

Matilda

The Matilda served through the entire war. Most vehicles mounted a 2pdr (40mm/1.57in) gun and could engage enemy tanks, but a proportion mounted a 3in (76mm) howitzer and were intended for the close support role.

A USEFUL CHASSIS

The Matilda was developed as an infantry tank. It was intended to move at the pace of the infantrymen it was supporting, and did not need a long range for its intended role. This philosophy made the Matilda design unsuitable for the mobile warfare it found itself conducting in North Africa. In addition, although its defensive capabilities were impressive, the Matilda was slow to manufacture at a time when vast numbers were needed. Its armour was both expensive and complex to cast; this contributed to the need for alternative designs. Once replacements were available, the Matilda was withdrawn from front-line service and the chassis was used for various other purposes, including a mobile searchlight designed to blind enemy troops and pinpoint their positions, a bridgelayer, a flamethrower tank and engineering vehicles.

PzKpfw III

In the mid-1930s, the mainstay of German armoured forces was envisaged as a complimentary pair of vehicles. The Panzer III, as it came to be designated, would mount an anti-tank gun while the heavier Panzer IV would use a larger calibre, low-velocity gun for infantry support. Several early models of the Panzer III were tested and found to be flawed, and it was the virtually identical Ausf E and F versions that eventually went into production. These were better protected than earlier models and had improved suspension. Critically, they had a large turret ring capable of taking a 50mm (1.97in) gun. Panzer IIIs were available in small numbers of the 1940 invasion of France, and before this campaign was even over the Ausf G version, with more armour and a 50mm (1.97in) gun, had gone into production. The basic design was upgraded throughout the war, gaining a longer and more powerful gun as the Ausf J model. However, the Panzer III could be stretched only so far, and by the last years of the war it was no longer suitable for front-line combat.

- Medium tank with a crew of five
- Initial armament of 37mm (1.45in) gun upgraded to 50mm (1.97in)
- Basis for many other vehicles, including Sturmgeschütz III assault gun

SPECIFICATIONS

Country of Origin: *Germany*

Crew: *5*

Weight: *22,300kg (49,060lb)*

Dimensions: *Length 6.41m (21ft); width 2.95m (9ft 8in); height 2.50m (8ft 2.5in)*

Range: *175km (110 miles)*

Armour: *30mm (1.18in) (Ausf M version)*

Armament: *One 75mm (2.95in) L/24 gun; two 7.92mm (0.31in) machine gun*

Powerplant: *One Maybach HL 120 TRM 12-cylinder petrol engine developing 224kW (300hp)*

Performance: *Maximum road speed 40km/h (25mph); fording 0.8m (2ft 8in); vertical obstacle 0.6m (2ft); trench 2.59m (8ft 6in)*

7

7

PzKpfw III

The Panzer III had an unusually large crew for a medium tank (commander, gunner, loader, radio operator and driver). It was the first German tank to carry an intercom system, which allowed improved crew coordination.

OUTDATED IN 4 YEARS

The Inspector for Mechanized Troops originally wanted the Panzer III to mount a 50mm (1.97in) gun, but eventually a 37mm (1.45in) weapon was selected. This was largely because the same weapon was already in service as an infantry anti-tank gun. Using the same gun and ammunition would simplify production and logistics, and at the time the 37mm (1.45in) seemed entirely adequate for the anti-tank role. However, as the war progressed it became obvious that a more powerful gun was necessary to take on better-protected enemy tanks. Such was the pace of progress that a tank which was just becoming available in 1940 had reached the end of its usefulness by 1944 despite repeated upgrades. The design continued to be influential, however: several US tanks, including the M24 Chaffee and M26 Pershing, were strongly influenced by studies of captured PzKpfw IIIs.

PzKpfw IV

The Panzer IV Ausf A appeared in 1937. It was built around several common components with the Panzer III, and had the same engine. It was significantly longer, however, with eight road wheels instead of the Panzer III's six. Its intended role was fire support, engaging anti-tank guns and enemy strongpoints in support of infantry or other tanks. Early models (A–E) incorporated various modifications, and were deployed for the invasion of France in 1940. Experience led to a redesign that became the Ausf F1 model, appearing in 1941. The Ausf F1 still mounted a short gun, making it ineffective against enemy tanks, and almost immediately after the F1 had gone into production the Ausf F2 version appeared. The Ausf F2 carried a long – and much more powerful – 75mm (2.95in) gun capable of penetrating tank armour. This trend continued with the Ausf G, whose later models had an even longer gun. Gaining a tank-killing armament enabled the Panzer IV to become a general-purpose battle tank rather than a specialized support vehicle, and it was in this role that the Panzer IV served for the rest of the war.

- Medium tank with a crew of five
- Progressed from a fire-support vehicle to a battle tank
- Chassis used as the basis for many other vehicles

SPECIFICATIONS

Country of Origin: *Germany*

Crew: *5*

Weight: *25,000kg (55,000lb)*

Dimensions: *Length 7.02m (23ft); width 3.29m (10ft 9.5in); height 2.68m (8ft 9.5in)*

Range: *200km (125 miles)*

Armour: *50–60mm (1.97–2.4in)*

Armament: *(Ausf H version) one 75mm (2.95in) gun; two 7.92mm (0.31in) MG34 machine guns*

Powerplant: *One Maybach HL 120 TRM 12-cylinder petrol engine developing 224kW (300hp)*

Performance: *Maximum road speed 38km/h (24mph); fording 1m (3ft 3in); vertical obstacle 0.6m (2ft 11in); trench 2.20m (7ft 3in)*

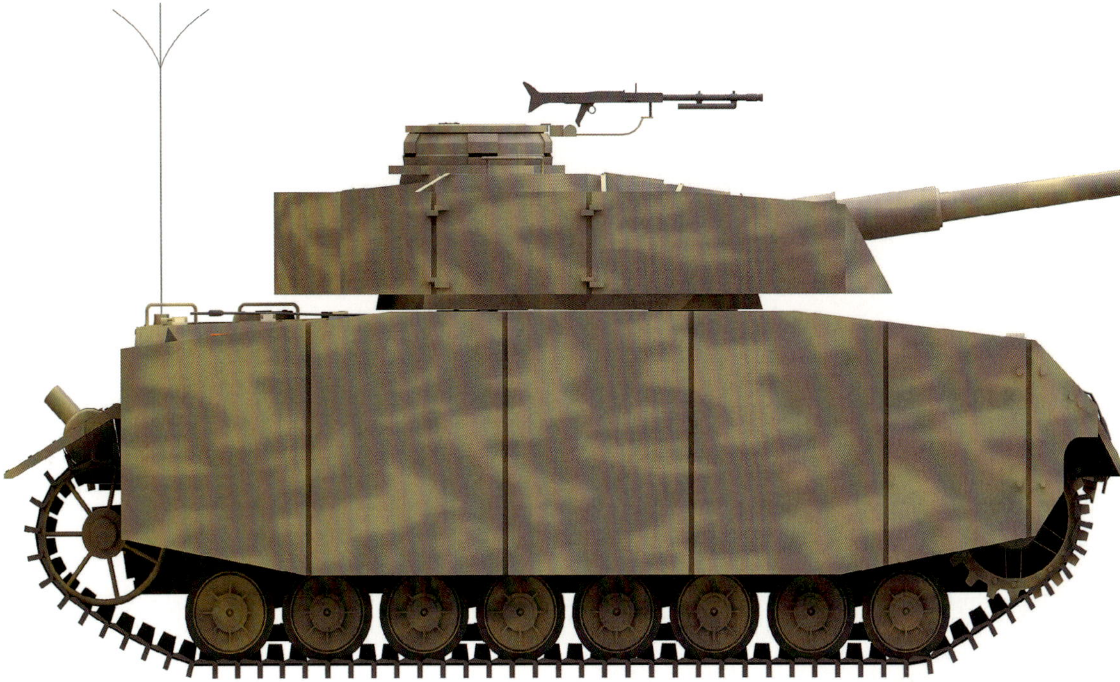

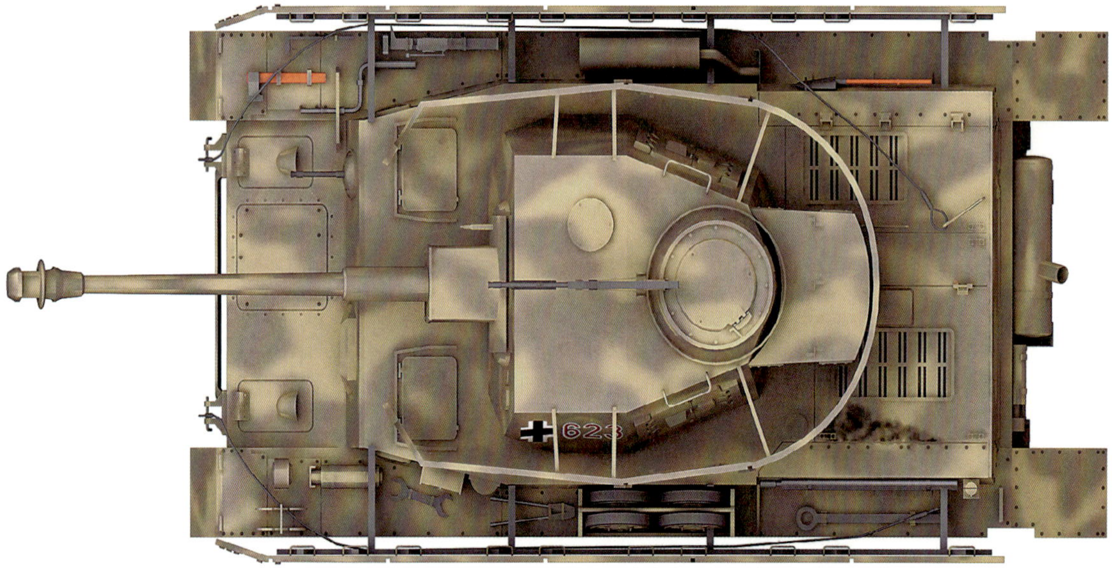

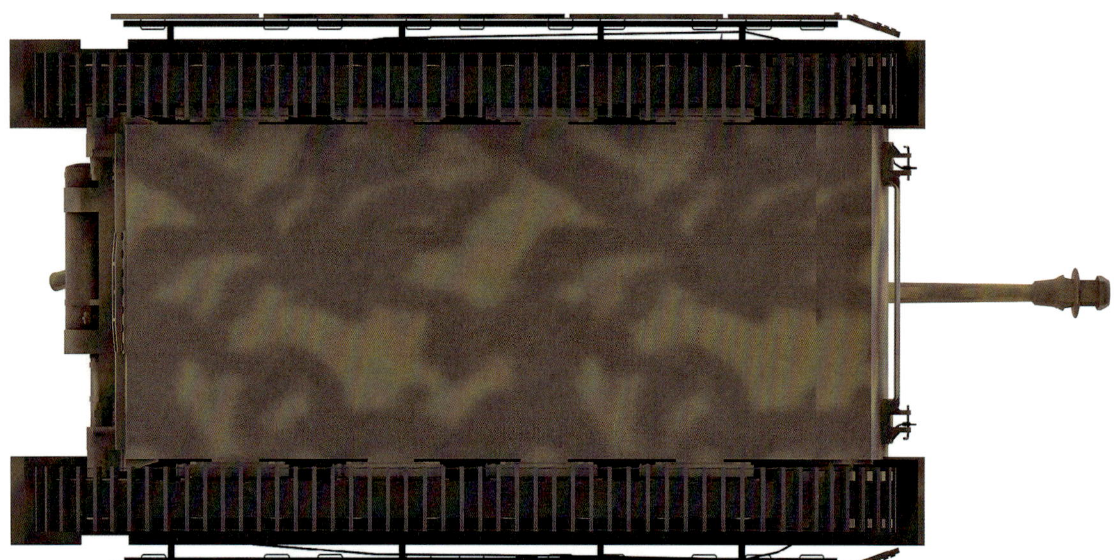

PzKpfw IV
Among the variations that appeared during the war were side skirts of steel plate. These were intended to defeat shaped-charge anti-tank weapons by causing the warhead to detonate short of the tank's armour.

PROVEN WORKHORSE

Early Panzer IVs mounted a short 75mm (2.95in) gun, which fired high-explosive rounds or sometimes smoke rounds. An anti-armour projectile was available, but was not effective against well-armoured tanks. The high-velocity gun of later models remained a credible threat to Allied tanks for the entire war. Later models also incorporated features designed to simplify and speed up production, which was necessary due to the immense demand for tanks from both the German army and allied forces. Arguably, Germany might have been well advised to concentrate on production of the proven and effective workhorse that was the PzKpfw IV rather than expending huge resources on the more impressive but complex Panther and Tiger. These heavy tanks were expensive to develop and slow to build, absorbing resources that could have been put into making large numbers of Panzer IVs.

T-34/85

The original T-34 tank, equipped with a 76mm (3in) gun, was a revolutionary design. With sloped armour and a small silhouette to increase survivability, the T-34 represented a balance of mobility, protection and firepower. However, by 1943, Axis tanks capable of defeating the T-34 were taking the field, and an upgrade became necessary. Soviet doctrine required that the T-34 fulfil a wide range of roles. The T-34/85 was primarily created to carry a more powerful 85mm (3.35in) gun capable of taking on the Panthers and Tigers that had tipped the balance – in terms of quality – against the Soviets. The new gun required a larger turret, enabling a loader to be added to the crew. The original T-34 was designed in part for rapid construction, and changing over to the new version was possible without undue disruption because it was a natural evolution of the T-34/76. The new model featured thicker armour and an improved gearbox but the chassis and powerplant were otherwise little changed. There was no need for a vast period of development; instead the T-34/85 went smoothly into production and reached the battlefield quickly.

- Medium tank with a crew of five
- Powerful 85mm (3.35in) main gun
- Retained the T-34's excellent mobility and protection

SPECIFICATIONS

Country of Origin: *Soviet Union*

Crew: *5*

Weight: *32,000kg (70,560lb)*

Dimensions: *Length 6m (19ft 7in); width 3m (9ft 9in); height 2.6m (8ft 6in)*

Range: *360km (223 miles)*

Armour: *75mm (2.95in)*

Armament: *One 85mm (3.35in) ZiS-S-53 cannon; two 7.62mm (0.3in) machine guns*

Powerplant: *One V-2 V-12 cylinder 493hp (372kW) diesel engine*

Performance: *Maximum speed: 55km/h (33mph)*

Л
170a

Л
170a

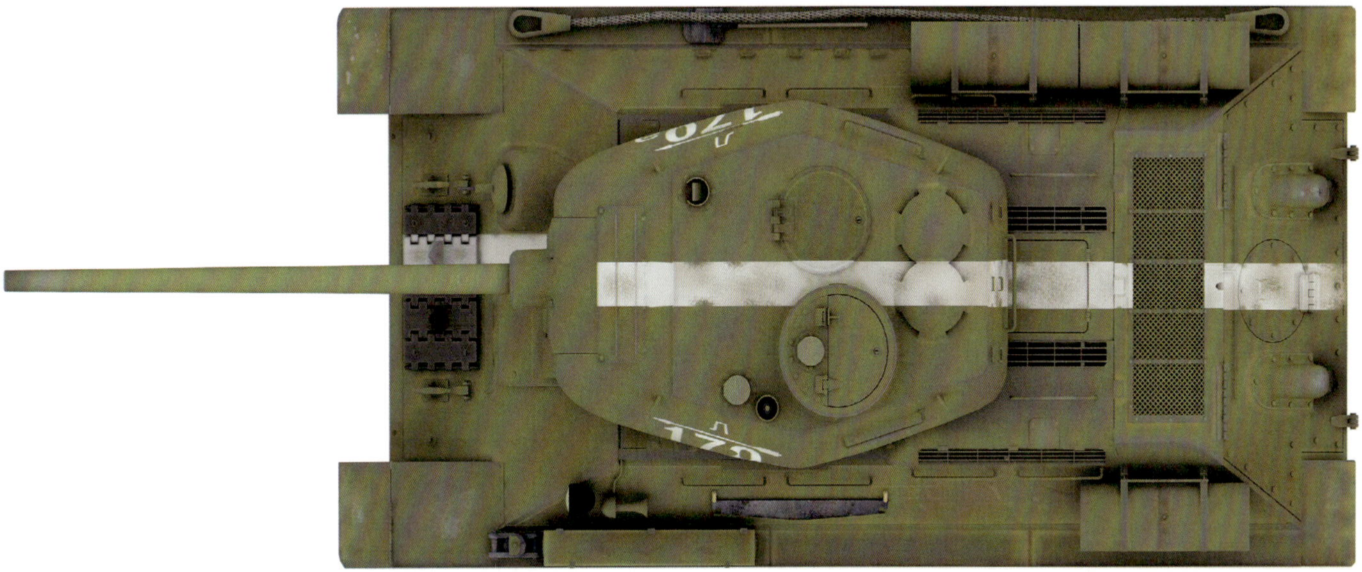

T-34/85

The T-34's lineage is apparent from the arrangement of its road wheels. The Christie suspension system was well proven by the time the T-34/85 was designed, and the designers saw no reason to try to innovate at a time when speed of production was paramount.

MAIN GUN PROBLEMS

Whereas some nations chose to develop several tank designs, all with their own specialist niche, the Soviet Union wanted a single tank that could tackle the new generation of Axis tanks and fulfil whatever other roles presented themselves. A developed version of the T-34 was the obvious solution. However, it proved more difficult than expected to fit the 85mm (3.35in) gun chosen for the T-34/85 into its turret. It was adapted from an anti-aircraft weapon, as were many tank and anti-tank guns, and while mounting problems were ironed out, the T-35/85 was given an alternate weapon. For tanks like the T-35/85, which had a long gun that projected well forward of the tank, it was common practice to traverse it to the rear when travelling in areas where combat was not expected.

Sherman

At the outbreak of World War II, the US military needed to acquire a large armoured force quickly. To this end, the M3 (Lee, or Grant) tank was put into production. The M3 was conceived to get a 75mm (2.95in) gun onto the armoured battlefield as soon as possible, but it carried this gun in a hull mount, which limited its effectiveness in combat. The turret-mounted 37mm (1.45in) gun was capable of all-round fire but was inadequate to take on the German Panzers. The M4 (Sherman) was developed from the M3, using a modified chassis and a cast turret mounting a 75mm (2.95in) gun. Deliveries of the M4A1 began in January 1942, with the tank seeing action later that year. Experience in combat showed that the Sherman was poorly protected and had a tendency to catch fire when hit, but was nevertheless an effective combat tank. Field modifications included appliqué armour to protect the vulnerable ammunition stowage and sandbags to defeat infantry anti-armour weapons. New models also appeared, with improvements to the hull, armour or powerplant. The most notable variant was the Sherman 'Firefly', mounting a 17pdr (76 mm/2.3in) gun.

- Medium tank with a crew of five
- 75mm (2.95in) or larger gun could defeat most enemy tanks
- Protection somewhat light compared to equivalent designs

SPECIFICATIONS

Country of Origin: *USA*

Crew: *5*

Weight: *32,284kg (71,024lb)*

Dimensions: *Length, with gun 7.52m (24ft 8in), and over hull 6.27m (20ft 7in); width 2.68m (8ft 9.5in); height 3.43m (11ft 2.875in)*

Range: *161km (100 miles)*

Armour: *15–100mm (0.59–3.94in)*

Armament: *One 75mm (2.95in) gun; two 7.62mm (0.3in) machine guns*

Powerplant: *One Ford GAA V-8 petrol engine developing 335.6kW or 373kW (400hp or 500hp)*

Performance: *Maximum road speed 47km/h (29mph); fording 0.91m (3ft); vertical obstacle 0.61m (2ft); trench 2.26m (7ft 5in)*

US.ARMY
3066192

US.ARMY
3066192

Sherman

The M4 Sherman was used as the basis for various specialist vehicles, including mine-clearance tanks and amphibious variants. Less common were heavily armoured 'Jumbo' assault tanks and a version with a 105mm (4.1in) gun.

75223-Y

BEATING THE ODDS

Although the M4 Sherman was not as individually awesome as a Panther or Tiger, it was a better weapon for war-fighting. Designed to be built and deployed in vast numbers, it carried a powerful armament into action and offered adequate protection to its crew. It was estimated that it took four or five Shermans to eliminate a Tiger, and that only one Sherman would survive the encounter. However, there were vastly more than four Shermans to each Tiger, and there were other ways to level the odds. Some Shermans were armed with the British 17pdr (76.2mm/3in) gun, which offered superior performance against armour than the standard 76mm (3in) gun. Tanks carrying the 17pdr (76.2mm/3in) gun were given the designation 'Firefly'. Mixed formations of three standard M4 Shermans and one Firefly were used later in the war.

Panther

No sooner had the Panzer III/IV partnership gone into production than studies began to develop an improved battle tank, although this project was not urgent at first. However, tank-versus-tank clashes during the 1941 invasion of the Soviet Union demonstrated that a new design was urgently needed to counter the impressive T-34. The Panzer V programme became priority, and a design was rushed into production before testing was complete. As a result, the new tank, named Panther, suffered from teething troubles when it was first deployed for combat. Its shortcomings were demonstrated in the battles around Kursk in 1943, with breakdowns common in the harsh Russian conditions. Improved versions of the Panther eliminated most of its mechanical troubles. The Panther Ausf G variant was given additional armour protection and improved power train, including better exhaust handling. This variant first appeared in March 1944. Another upgraded model, designated out of sequence as Ausf F, was not ready by the end of the war. The Panther developed into a formidable vehicle, which many experts consider to be overall the best tank of the war.

- Medium tank with a crew of five
- Powerful 75mm (2.95in) gun
- Sloped armour offered very good protection

SPECIFICATIONS

Country of Origin: *Germany*

Crew: *5*

Weight: *45,500kg (100,100lb)*

Dimensions: *Length 8.86m (29ft 0.75in); width 3.43m (11ft 3in); height 3.10m (10ft 2in)*

Range: *177km (110 miles)*

Armour: *30–110mm (1.2–4.3in)*

Armament: *One 75mm (2.95in) gun; three 7.92mm (0.31in) MG34 machine guns (one coaxial, one anti-aircraft, one on hull front)*

Powerplant: *One Maybach HL 230 12-cylinder diesel developing 522kW (700hp) maximum*

Performance: *Road speed 46km/h (29mph); fording 1.70m (5ft 7in); vertical obstacle 0.91m (3ft); trench 1.91m (6ft 3in)*

200
VI
V
IV
III
II
I

200
I
II
III
IV
V
VI

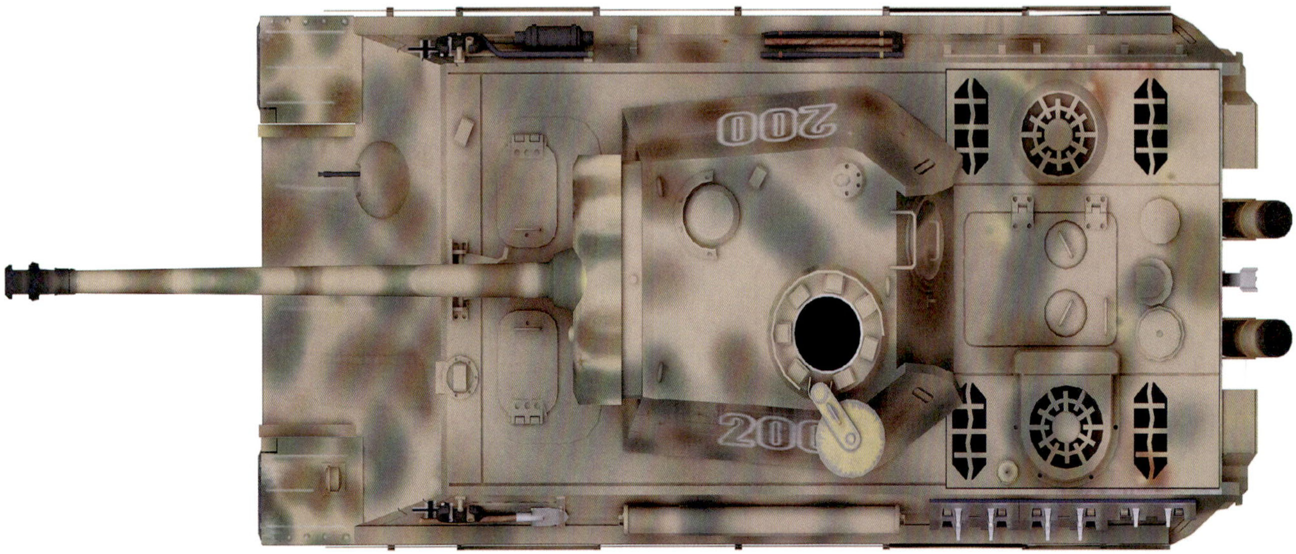

Panther

Some German designers were so impressed by the T-34 that they suggested a direct copy should be made as Germany's next battle tank. This was not acceptable, but several features of the Soviet design were incorporated into the Panther. These included sloped armour and wide tracks.

HARSH ENVIRONMENTS

The appearance of the Panther was significantly different to other German tanks of World War II. Its sloped armour was a concept 'borrowed' from the Soviet T-34, and increased the protection offered by the same thickness of armour. This was partly by creating the possibility that an armour-piercing round might glance off, but sloped armour also increased the effective thickness of metal that a projectile had to penetrate in order to reach the tank's interior. Along with the Tiger, the Panther used overlapping road wheels, which reduced ground pressure and enhanced mobility in rough terrain. This seemed like a good idea in theory, but the wheels were prone to clogging with mud (which, in Russia, would often freeze solid) and were complex to repair if damaged.

Cromwell

Britain produced a series of cruiser tanks during World War II. The Centaur, built to meet specification A27L, was modestly successful and its chassis was used as the basis of the Cromwell (A27M) cruiser tank. Many early Cromwells were converted Centaurs. Most notably, the Cromwell used the Rolls-Royce Meteor engine, the same powerplant as the Spitfire fighter. Its armament was upgraded from the 57mm (2.24in) of the Centaur to 75mm (2.95in), usually by reboring 57mm guns. Late in its career the Cromwell received the powerful 17pdr (76.2mm/3in) gun, able to penetrate the heaviest German tanks. The Cromwell brought together a powerful engine and a big enough gun to take on the German Panzers, protected by reasonably thick armour. An improved Christie suspension provided good cross-country mobility. The armament was versatile enough to engage tanks with armour-piercing ammunition and to fire high-explosive rounds for infantry support. Although not as effective as the best German tanks, the Cromwell was good enough to stand a chance against them and was built in the largest numbers of any wartime British tank.

- Medium (cruiser) tank with a crew of five
- Good balance of weaponry and mobility
- Most numerous British tank of the war

SPECIFICATIONS

Country of Origin: *United Kingdom*

Crew: *5*

Weight: *27,942kg (61,472lb)*

Dimensions: *Length 6.42m (21ft 0.75in); width 3.048m (10ft); height 2.51m (8ft 3in)*

Range: *278km (173 miles)*

Armour: *8–76mm (0.3–2.9in)*

Armament: *One 75mm (2.95in) gun; one coaxial 7.62mm (0.3in) machine gun*

Powerplant: *One Rolls-Royce Meteor V-12 petrol engine developing 425kW (570hp)*

Performance: *Maximum speed 61km/h (38mph); fording 1.219m (4ft); vertical obstacle 0.914m (3ft); trench 2.286 (7ft 6in)*

Cromwell
The Cromwell's distinctive turret, with its prominent bolts, resulted from its method of construction. Armour plate was bolted to the outside of a boxlike internal structure. Some later models were welded rather than bolted, speeding up construction.

A SWIFT MOVER

The distinctive big-wheel Christie suspension used by many British cruiser tanks was adopted after officials were impressed by Soviet tanks that used it. Robust and reliable, the Christie system gave good service in a range of environments, from frozen plains through seas of mud to the North African desert. The combination of excellent suspension and a powerful engine made the Cromwell one of the fastest Allied tanks of the war, whilst allowing it to be an effective gun platform even on rough terrain. However, the gun itself gave a lot of trouble on early models, and it was not until the middle of 1944 that the Cromwell finally began to achieve its potential. Even then it was outmatched by the best German tanks, but not so much so that it could not defeat them if well handled.

Comet

The Comet (design specification A34) Cruiser Tank was the product of a development process that began with the A27 Centaur. The Centaur was modestly successful and its chassis was used as the basis of the Cromwell, which in turn was developed into the Comet. The Comet arrived late in the war, and did not play any significant combat role. However, it represented the culmination of years of experience against the German panzers, and was the first British tank capable of taking on a Panther one-to-one. The Comet retained the best aspects of its predecessors, including the Rolls-Royce Meteor engine, the same powerplant as the Spitfire fighter. However, other features were significantly redesigned. An improved suspension enabled high-speed, albeit rough, transit of broken terrain. Armament was also improved, using a compact version of the proven 17pdr (76.2mm/3in) gun, designated Vickers HV (for High Velocity) 75mm (2.95in); this was lighter and easier to handle but almost identical in performance. The Comet was designed with lessons learned in the war in mind.

- Medium (cruiser) tank with a crew of five
- Excellent gun in electrically-traversed turret
- Designed to tackle the best German tanks of the later war

SPECIFICATIONS

Country of Origin: *United Kingdom*

Crew: *5*

Weight: *32,223kg (71,051lb)*

Dimensions: *Length 6.5m (21ft 6in); width 3m (10ft 1in); height 2.67m (8ft 6in)*

Range: *250km (155 miles)*

Armour: *25–102mm (0.98–4in)*

Armament: *1 x 76.2mm (3in) 17-pounder gun; two 7.92mm (0.31in) Besa MGs*

Powerplant: *One Rolls-Royce Meteor V-12 petrol engine developing 447kW (600hp)*

Performance: *Maximum speed 50km/h (32mph)*

T 330584

T 330584

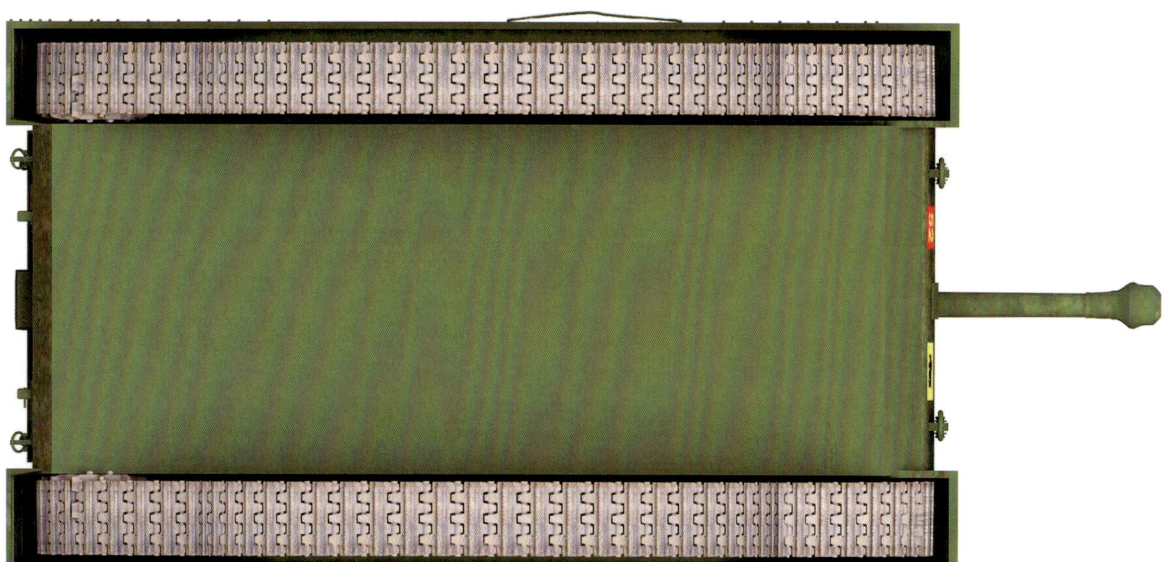

Comet

The Comet's road wheels give a clue to its lineage, through the Cromwell and earlier British cruiser tanks all the way back to Christie's inter-war designs. Its suspension worked well but gave the crew an unpleasant ride.

DECADES OF SERVICE

The Comet serves as an indication of where wartime British tank design was headed. It was designed for speed and high-mobility operations, having finally left behind the concept of the tank as an infantry support vehicle. It was still quite capable of operating with infantry, of course, and experience in Normandy in 1944 had showed that there were times when close cooperation was essential to the survival of the tank. The Comet was thus fitted with exhaust cowls that not only allowed infantry to ride safely on the engine deck but also reduced the chances of hot exhausts being spotted during night operations. However, it was not an unqualified success; its weak belly armour made the vehicle vulnerable to mines. Nevertheless, the Comet continued to serve through the 1960s and even into the 1970s.

KV-I

Development of the KV-I heavy tank began in 1938, as a replacement for the flawed multi-turret KT-35. It went into production in 1940 and was available in modest numbers to oppose the German invasion in 1941. Although its main gun was no heavier than that of the T-34, the KV-I had very thick armour and proved resilient on the battlefield. It was virtually invulnerable to most German anti-tank weapons, with only the heaviest anti-tank guns standing any chance of a penetrating hit. There are reports of KV-Is remaining in action after taking more than 50 hits, while its gun could penetrate any tank in the enemy arsenal. However, the KV-I was difficult to drive and operate, and mechanical breakdowns were frequent. Moreover, improved German anti-armour weapons were soon fielded which could deal with KV-Is, necessitating an upgrade to its armour. This resulted in transmission problems and rendered the tank underpowered. The KV-I was no match for the Tiger and the Panther but it remained a potent force. The shift from short-range defensive operations to major offensives caused the KV-I to be gradually retired.

- Heavy tank with a crew of five
- Poorly laid-out interior reduced efficiency
- Extremely heavy armour for the period, but soon matched by enemy anti-tank weapons

SPECIFICATIONS

Country of Origin: *Soviet Union*

Crew: *5*

Weight: *43,000kg (94,600lb)*

Dimensions: *Length 6.68m (21ft 11in); width 3.32m (10ft 10.7in); height 2.71m (8ft 10.7in)*

Range: *150km (93.2 miles)*

Armour: *100mm (3.94in)*

Armament: *One 76.2mm (3in) gun; three 7.62mm (0.3in) machine guns*

Powerplant: *One V-2K V-12 diesel engine developing 448kW (600hp)*

Performance: *Maximum (rarely achieved) road speed 35km/h (21.75mph); fording not known; vertical obstacle 1.20m (3ft 8in); trench 2.59m (8ft 6in)*

KV-I

The KV-I's lack of mobility caused a lightened version (KV-IS) to be developed. This tank later received an 85mm (3.35in) gun but retained most of the original design's mechanical flaws.

34-18
За Родину!

DESIGN FLAWS

The KV-I was visually very impressive but suffered from some serious flaws. The first was the difficulty of driving it; drivers quickly became exhausted from wrestling with the controls. Even when the transmission did not break down, some early models frequently required the application of a hammer in order to change gear. On top of this, the interior was awkwardly laid out, with crew efficiency further impaired by the dual function of the commander as loader for the main gun. The gun itself was entirely adequate during the early war, but improvements in German tank armour caused the KV-I to become less effective. Despite these problems it was a very tough combatant and was important during the battles of 1941–42 to stem the German invasion.

KV-II

Using the same hull and powerplant as the KV-I, the KV-II was an 'artillery tank' armed with a 152mm (6in) howitzer. It was intended as an assault gun, eliminating enemy strongpoints in support of an advance, or acting as a 'breakthrough tank' for heavy shock effect. Mounting such a large gun required a specially designed turret, which gave the KV-II its high silhouette. The turret suffered from numerous flaws due to its weight and size. The tank was also very slow because it was powered by the same engine as the KV-I but weighed much more. The KV-II normally used high-explosive shells in its main gun. Armour-piercing shells were not practical, as the high propellant charge would jam the turret due to recoil. Naval semi-armour-piercing shells could be used but were rarely available. The KV-II was a formidable opponent in the defensive role, acting as a mobile pillbox. Extremely hard to destroy, their heavy guns were capable of destroying most targets. However, the KV-II suffered from poor mobility and could be immobilized by shooting off the tracks. Many were also lost to breakdowns, and it was retired by the end of 1942.

- Heavy tank with a crew of six
- Armed with a 152mm (6in) howitzer
- Well armoured but mechanically defective

SPECIFICATIONS

Country of Origin: *Soviet Union*

Crew: *6*

Weight: *53,100kg (24,086lb)*

Dimensions: *Length 6.79m (22ft 3in); width 3.32m (10ft 11in); height 3.65m (12ft)*

Range: *140km (87 miles)*

Armour: *Up to 110mm (4.33in)*

Armament: *One 152mm (6in) and three 7.62mm (0.3in) machine guns*

Powerplant: *One V-2K V-12 diesel engine developing 410kW (550hp)*

Performance: *Maximum road speed 26km/h (16mph)*

Фор мать россиа

Фор мать россиа

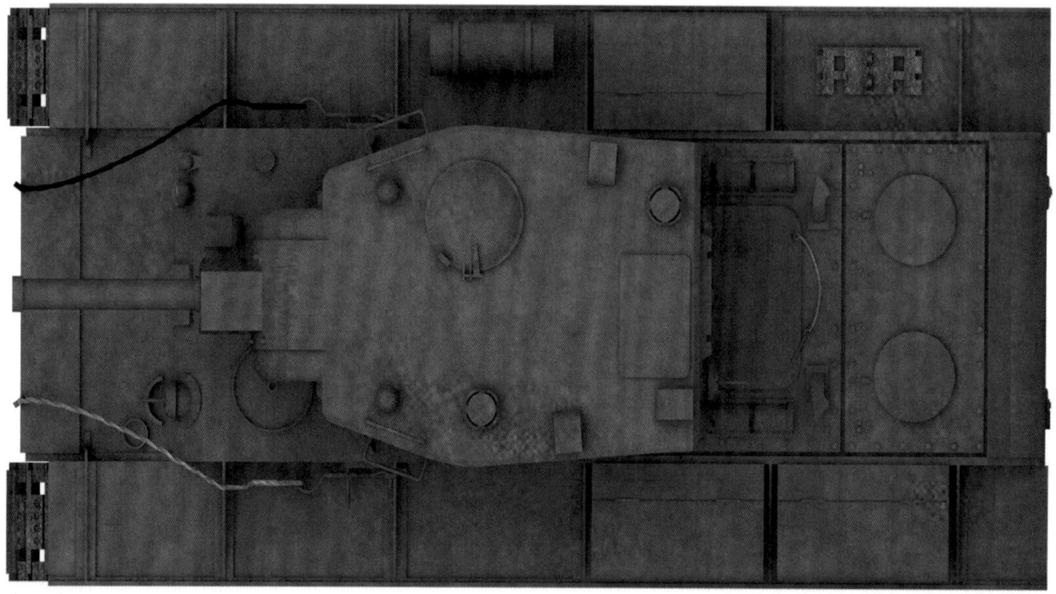

KV-II

Initial tests of the KV-II against bunkers on the Mannerheim Line in Finland were very promising. The heavily armoured tank could bring its main gun into killing range of bunkers with relative impunity.

TOUGH BUT FLAWED

The high silhouette of the KV-II's turret is apparent when compared to the armoured car in the foreground. This made it an easy target, which was compensated for by the tank's incredible toughness. A lone KV-II was able to prevent an entire Panzer division from advancing for a whole day near Leningrad, shrugging off dozens of direct hits. The only weapon capable of penetrating its armour was the 88mm (3.5in) anti-tank/anti-aircraft gun, though German gunners eventually learned to shoot off the tracks and thus make the tank vulnerable to infantry assault. The KV-II's limited operational range and low speed were acceptable in a bunker-busting assault vehicle but represented a severe drawback in mobile operations. As a result the design was phased out after less than 400 had been constructed.

Tiger

The PzKpfw VI Tiger was conceived in 1937 as a heavy 'breakthrough' tank intended to spearhead assaults against enemy positions. It was originally to have a 75mm (2.95in) gun, but this was uprated to an 88mm (3.5in) weapon derived from the lethal '88' anti-tank gun. The latter had, like many anti-armour guns, started out as an anti-aircraft gun. Mobility was a problem for such a large and heavy tank; the only feasible way to move Tigers any distance was by rail. The engine proved fuel-hungry, which was a problem later in the war when supplies were limited. The Tiger first saw action near Leningrad in August 1942, and was difficult to disable. Most anti-tank guns could penetrate only the hull sides and rear, and then from short range. This gave the Tigers a significant advantage, which was partially offset by their lack of mobility and small numbers. Throughout its career the Tiger proved formidable and acquired a legend of invulnerability. There were few variant models. The most famous is the Tiger II, or King Tiger, which was heavier than the Tiger I and used the same engine, reducing the design's already limited mobility.

- Heavy tank with a crew of five
- Potent 88mm (3.5in) gun capable of firing armour-piercing or explosive rounds
- Extremely thick (but not sloped) armour

SPECIFICATIONS

Country of Origin: *Germany*

Crew: *5*

Weight: *55,000kg (121,000lb)*

Dimensions: *Length 8.24m (27ft); width 3.73m (12ft 3in); height 2.86m (9ft 3.25in)*

Range: *100km (62 miles)*

Armour: *25–100mm (1–3.94in)*

Armament: *One 88mm (3.5in) KwK 36 gun; two 7.92 coaxial MG 34 machine guns*

Powerplant: *One Maybach HL 230 P45 12-cylinder petrol engine developing 522kW (700hp)*

Performance: *Maximum road speed 38km/h (24mph); fording 1.20m (3ft 11in); vertical obstacle 0.79m (2ft 7in); trench 1.8m (5ft 11in)*

712
712

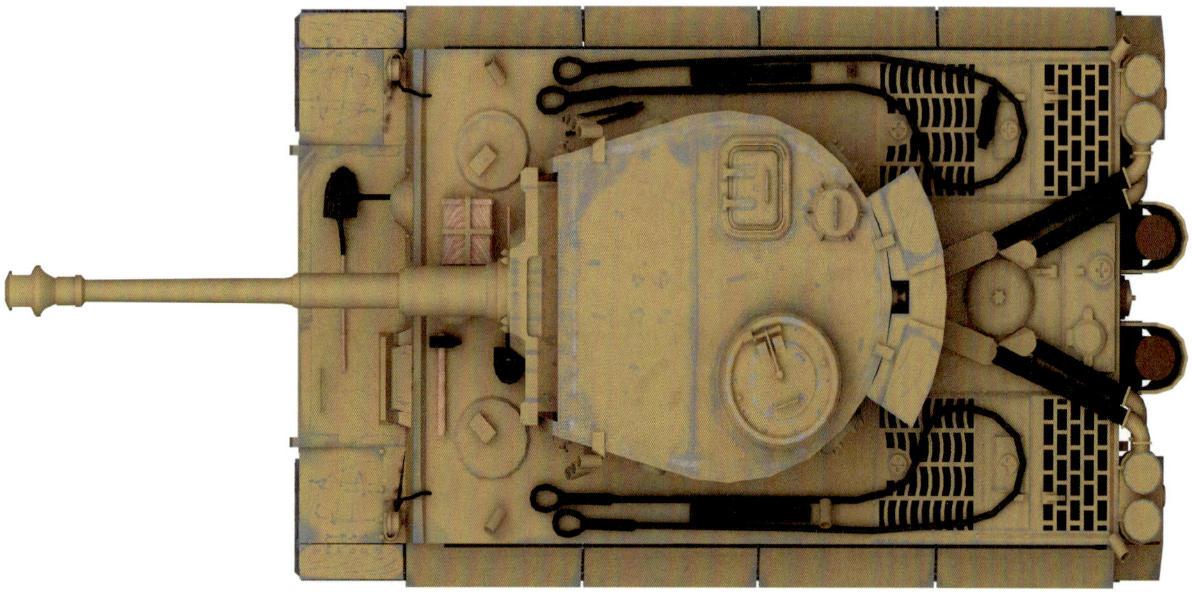

Tiger
The Tiger's wide tracks reduced ground pressure and improved mobility, but made it too wide for the standard railway gauge. Narrow 'travelling' tracks could be used on the inner road wheels only, with the outer ones removed to allow the tank to be carried by rail.

DEFENSIVE OPERATIONS

The Tiger was an extremely dangerous opponent, but its reputation became inflated. This actually worked to the German army's advantage, as reports of a Tiger sighting could trigger what became known as 'Tiger Terror' among enemy troops. Many of these sighting reports were spurious – Tigers were never available in large numbers – but were so damaging to morale that some Allied commanders forbade the passing of sighting reports to their troops. The Tiger was not mobile enough for fast-moving tank warfare, but proved highly effective in defensive operations during the later war. Operating on interior lines, Tigers could act as mobile anti-tank emplacements or make devastating short-range counter-attacks. Overall the Tiger was a flawed design which, whilst individually potent, represented a squandering of resources that might have been better spent on producing much greater numbers of Panzer IVs.

206

KV-85

The KV-I heavy tank had become obsolete because its 76.2mm (3in) gun could penetrate its opponents at only very short range. A lightened KV-I, designated KV-1S, was available to provide the basis for an interim upgunned heavy tank until new designs were available. The KV-IS hull was mated to a turret designed for the IS-I tank that was still in development. This turret mounted an 85mm (3.35in) gun, fulfilling the firepower needs but also adding to the weight of the tank. The new tank, KV-85, was thus as heavy as the original KV-I had been before it was lightened to create the KV-IS, and suffered from similar mobility problems. Production, which began in late 1943, ran for just 130 examples. Difficulties in manufacturing the KV-85's gun contributed to its early demise, though it had always been envisaged as a stop-gap until the IS series became available. The IS-I was not built in great numbers but the IS-II was mass produced as the main late-war Soviet heavy tank, replacing earlier models such as the KV-85. Although relatively few were made, KV-85s saw action in 1944, and the turret was developed for the upgunned T-34/85.

- Heavy tank with a crew of five (later four)
- Interim design based on KV-I hull
- Turret was designed for the IS series of tanks

SPECIFICATIONS

Country of Origin: *Soviet Union*

Crew: *5 (later 4)*

Weight: *46,000kg (101,430lb)*

Dimensions: *Length 8.6m (28ft 2in); width 3.25m (10ft 8in); height 2.8m (9ft 2in)*

Range: *330km (205 miles)*

Armour: *40–90mm (1.6–3.5in)*

Armament: *One 85mm (3.35in) D-5T gun; two 7.62mm (0.3in) machine guns*

Powerplant: *One V-2 12-cylinder diesel engine developing 450kW (600hp)*

Performance: *Maximum road speed 42km/h (26mph)*

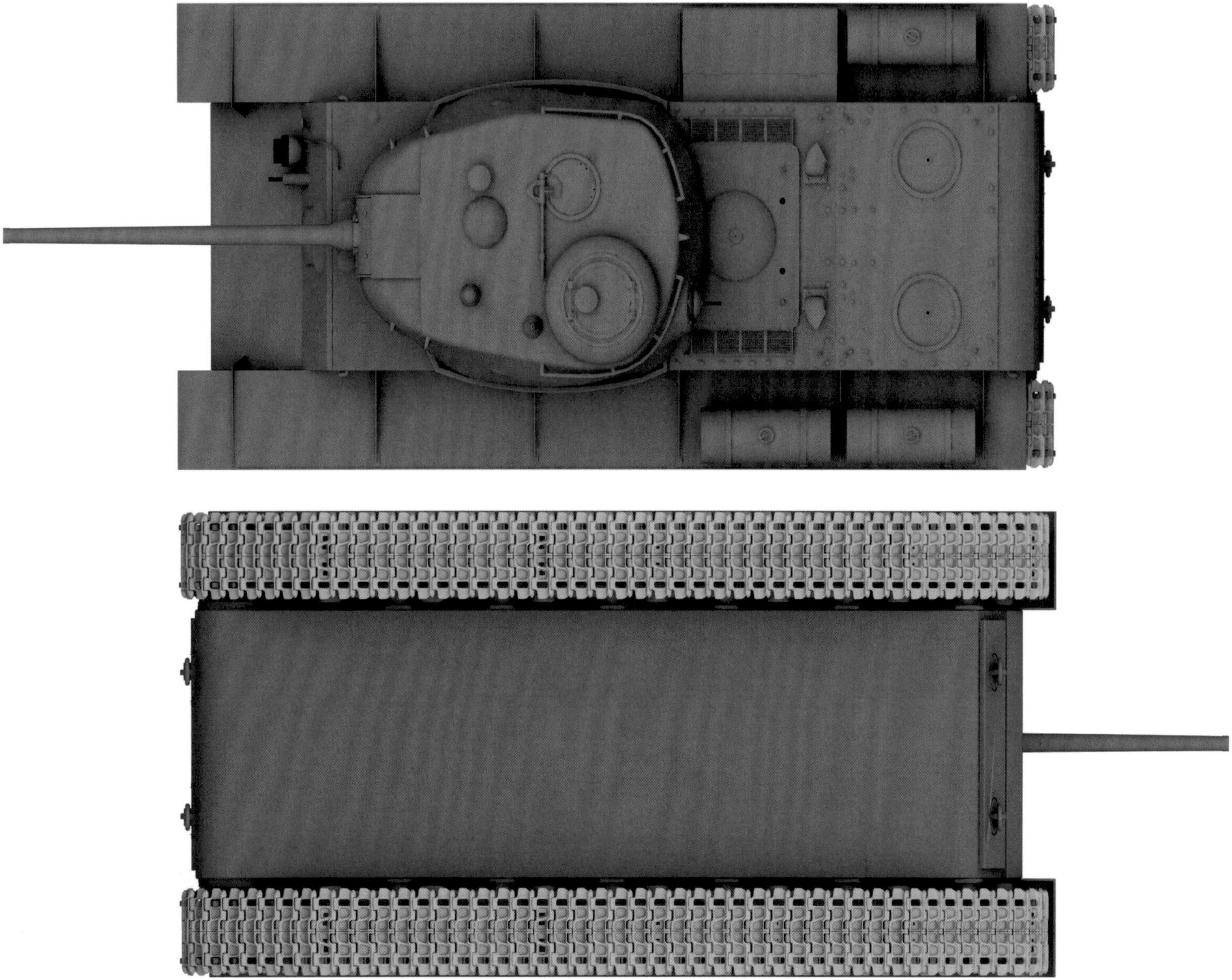

KV-85
The majority of KV-85s served in the Crimea and the Ukraine. They proved adequate in combat against Panthers and Tigers but possessed no great advantages. Their performance in action was thus somewhat mixed.

WEIGHT PROBLEMS

The main challenge facing the designers of the KV-85 was fitting an enlarged turret ring into the KV-IS hull. This was necessary if a larger gun were to be accommodated, so fillets were inserted into the hull to allow the larger turret to be mounted. The internal organization of the tank was altered after some experimentation, with the bow machine gunner/radio operator position deleted and the radio moved to the turret, where the commander could use it. The new turret was heavy, however, and this brought the weight of the tank back up to that of the KV-I before it was lightened to create the KV-IS. The end result was a tank with increased offensive capability, but at the price of reduced speed and mobility.

IS-2

The appearance of German heavy tanks made the existing KV-I design obsolete. While stop-gap measures were put in place, work began on the IS (Josef Stalin) series of tanks. These were based on a redesigned KV-I hull with a new turret. The IS-I appeared in 1943, with an improved transmission and powerplant over the KV-I, and a larger turret mounting an 85mm (3.35in) gun. Some were given a 100mm (3.94in) gun instead, but the IS-I was quickly supplanted by the IS-2. This version mounted a 122mm (4.8in) gun capable of shooting right through a Panther from front to back at over 1500m (4920ft). The IS-2 was sufficiently well armoured to withstand 88mm (3.5in) hits, but retained a good degree of mobility. The huge gun of the IS-2 was impressive, but the size of its projectiles made loading slow and limited capacity to 28 rounds. This was offset by its ability to engage from beyond the range of German 88mm (3.5in) and 75mm (2.95in) guns. Its gun could also fire HE projectiles for use against infantry positions in the breakthrough role. The IS-2 was usually deployed in the early stages of an offensive, smashing holes in enemy defences.

- Heavy tank with a crew of four
- Armed with 122mm (4.8in) main gun
- Capable of using anti-tank or high explosive ammunition for the support/breakthrough role

SPECIFICATIONS

Country of Origin: *Soviet Union*

Crew: *4*

Weight: *46,000kg (101,200lb)*

Dimensions: *Length 9.9m (32ft 5.8in); width 3.09m (10ft 1.6in); height 2.73m (8ft 11.5in)*

Range: *240km (149 miles)*

Armour: *132mm (5.2in)*

Armament: *One 122mm (4.8in) gun; one 12.7mm (0.5in) machine gun; one 7.62mm (0.3in) machine gun*

Powerplant: *One V-2-IS (V-2K) V-12 diesel developing 447kW (600hp)*

Performance: *Maximum road speed 37km/h (23mph); fording not known; vertical obstacle 1m (3ft 3in); trench 2.49m (8ft 2in)*

IS-2

The IS-2 was easier to drive than the KV series and had a more reliable transmission, although it was not much faster. The IS-2 was less prone to breakdown, which was a major factor in the loss rates of KV series tanks.

IMPROVED VISIBILITY

The IS-2 was developed in response to the appearance of German Panther and Tiger tanks on the Eastern Front, and proved an effective countermeasure. The IS series of tanks benefited from extensive redesign work, creating a reliable vehicle with a very potent weapon. Two possible guns were considered; a 100mm (3.94in) version and the 122mm (4.8in) that was finally chosen. This weapon was based on an already available artillery piece and proved capable of blowing the turret clean off an enemy tank. The IS-2 had to be built in large numbers, of course, and once the basic IS-2 design was ready it was simplified as much as possible. This led to a series of changes during production. Notably, later models received a redesigned bow and improvements to the crew's visibility when the tank was closed up for action.

Maus

Had the Maus project ever reached completion, it would have been by far the heaviest tank the world has ever seen. Development work began in 1941, possibly in response to Soviet heavy tank development. The initial version was to carry a 128mm (5in) gun and a co-axial 75mm (2.95in) weapon, with the possibility of a final armament up to 170mm (6.7in). Originally intended to weigh an incredible 100 tons (110 US tons), the Maus fell victim to Hitler's obsession with bigger projects. The final design weighed almost twice as much. Moving this vast amount of metal around required a powerplant that was simply not available, although efforts were made to build one. Weight caused many more technical problems, with the result that the initial order for 150 was cancelled in 1943. Development work continued up to the end of the war, however. Strategic mobility proved impossible – no bridge could take its immense weight, so a schnorkel system was developed to allow it to crawl across riverbeds. Work was also begun on a specially-designed rail transport car, but this progressed slowly. Without such a system, the Maus could not be deployed at all.

- Superheavy tank with a crew of five
- Co-axial 128mm (5in) and 75mm (2.95in) guns
- Heaviest tank design ever conceived

SPECIFICATIONS

Country of Origin: *Germany*

Crew: *5*

Weight: *200 metric tons (220 tons)*

Dimensions: *Length 10.2m (33ft 6in); width 3.71m (12ft 2in); height 3.63m (11ft 11in)*

Range: *160km (99 miles) (road); 62km (39 miles) (off road)*

Armour: *460mm (18in) (in the area of the mantlet); 240mm (9.4in) (turret front); 190mm (7in) (hull side and rear)*

Armament: *One 128mm (5in) KwK 44 gun L/55 (32 rounds)*

Powerplant: *One MB 517 diesel engine (V-shaped 12-cylinder) 895kW (1200hp)*

Performance: *Maximum road speed 13km/h (8.1mph)*

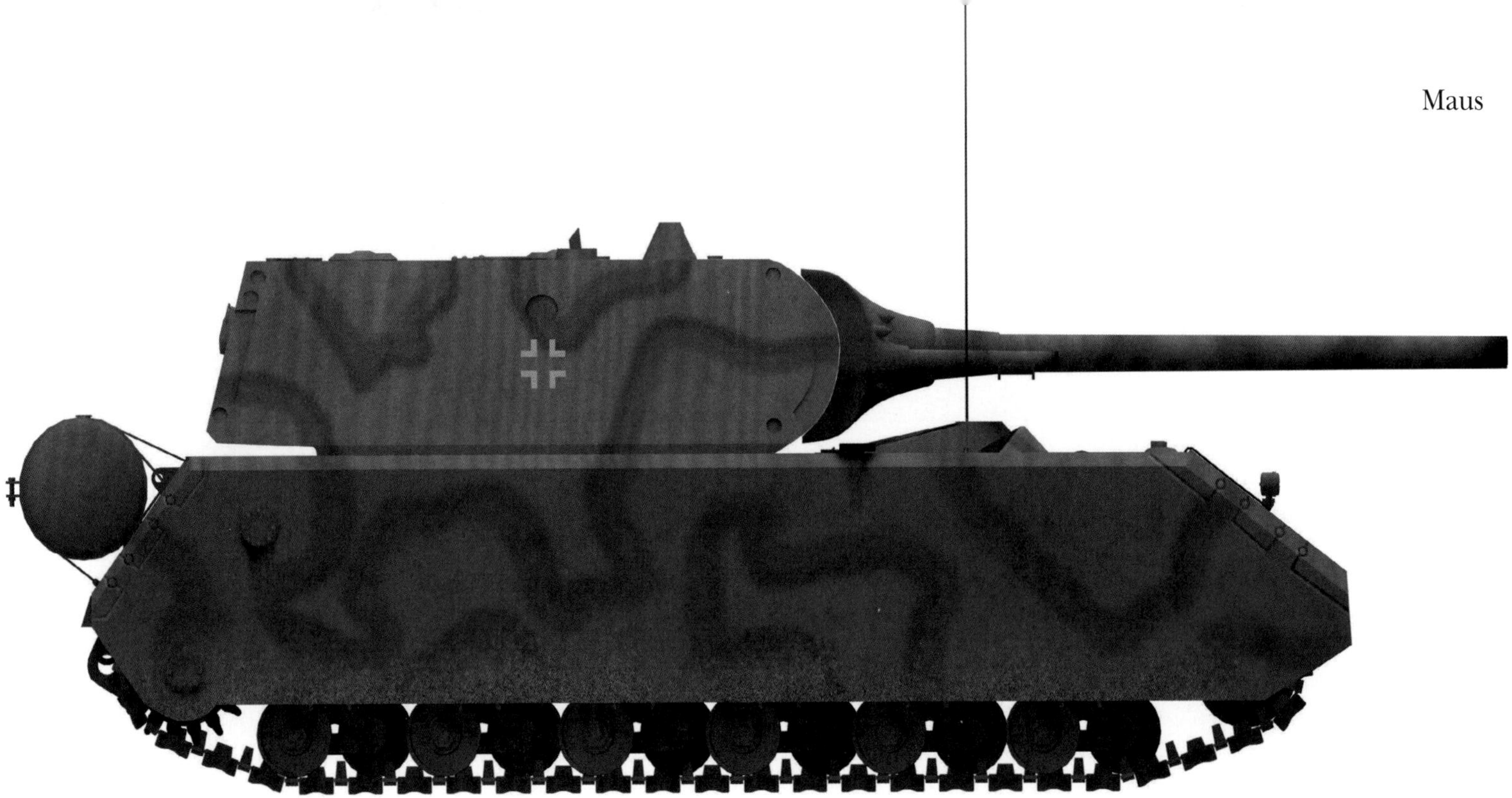

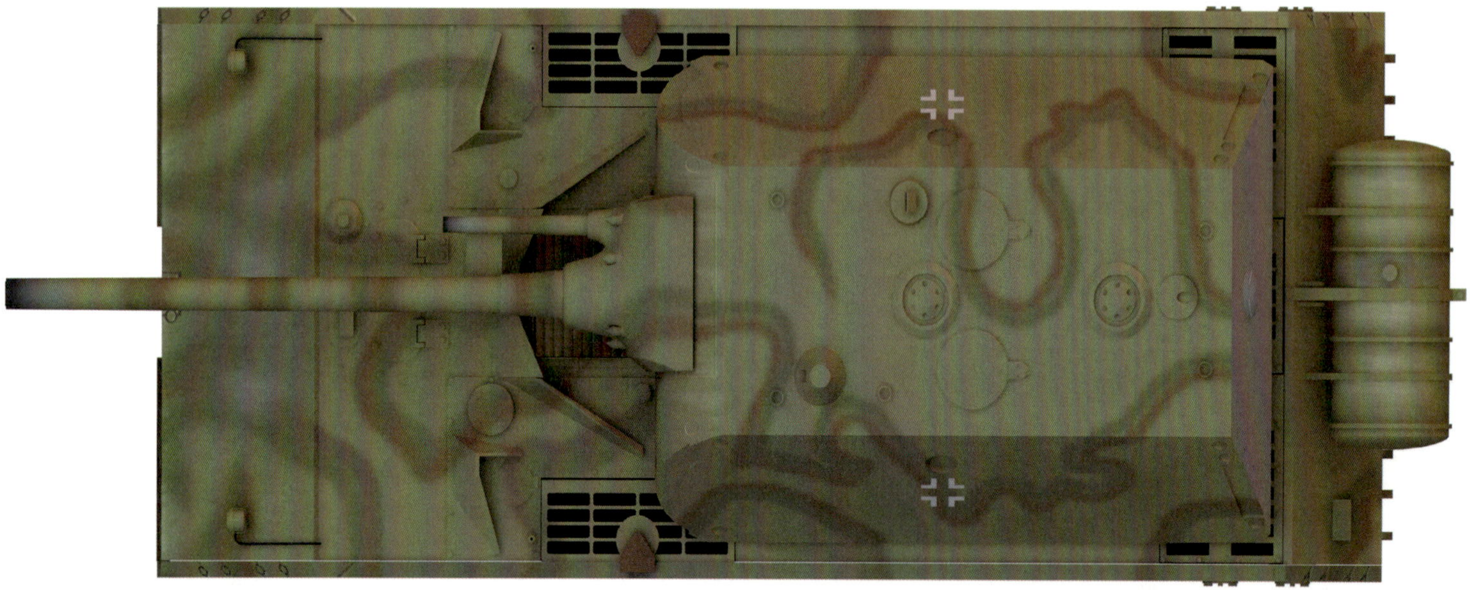

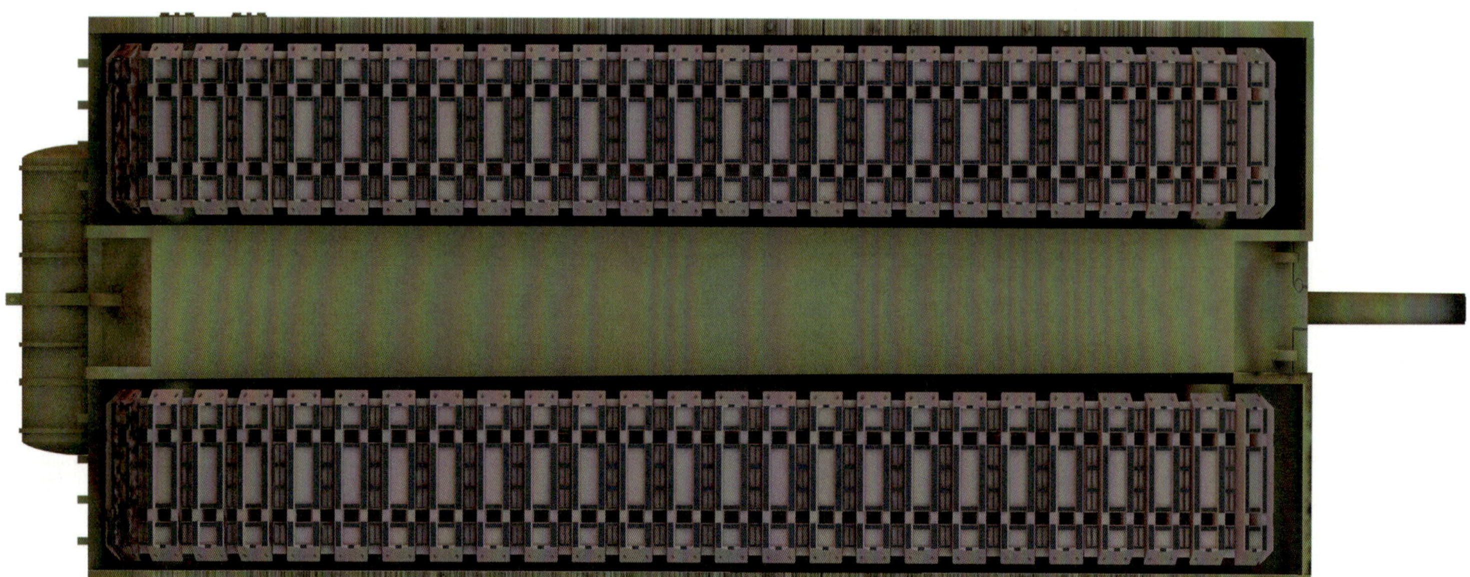

Maus

Tank design must balance three factors – firepower, mobility and protection. By emphasizing firepower and protection to an almost ridiculous extreme, the Maus made itself virtually immobile, and thus useless for its intended role.

MUSEUM PIECE

The Maus represented everything that was wrong with German wartime tank design. Rather than concentrate on workhorse designs which could be built in large numbers, Hitler demanded that vast resources be channelled into superweapon projects which had little chance of success. The Maus concept ran contrary to the Blitzkrieg *mode of warfare that was the German army's hallmark. Instead of a fast-moving assault, breakthrough and rampage in the enemy's rear, or a rapid armoured counter-attack based on speed and firepower, the Maus was designed to crawl slowly around the countryside acting as a semi-mobile fortress. A Maus was assembled from a hull and turret captured by the advancing Red Army, and today resides in the Museum of Armoured Forces near Moscow. It was tested by the Soviets in the 1950s but, not surprisingly, no attempt was made to build a similar vehicle.*

STuG III

The Sturmgeschütz (or STuG) III was built on the chassis of a Panzer III, armed with a short 75mm (2.95in) gun in a limited-traverse mounting. This weapon was excellent for fire support but limited when engaging enemy armour in the tank-destroyer role. Initial models gave good service during the invasion of France, but experience in combat resulted in necessary improvements. The Ausf F and the G model received a longer gun with a much higher muzzle velocity, and were produced from March 1942 until the end of the war. Earlier model STuG IIIs were refitted with long guns and additional armour. The more powerful gun enabled the STuG III to function as a tank destroyer, though this was a mixed blessing. A shortage of tanks caused assault guns to be incorporated into armoured formations, substituting for tanks in a role to which they were not suited. Like tank destroyers, assault guns are cheaper and simpler to produce than tanks. Used correctly, they increase the capabilities of infantry formations without weakening the armoured units. However, attempts to push assault guns into roles suited to tanks led to heavy losses.

- Assault gun with a crew of four
- Based on Panzer III chassis
- Later models received a longer gun and could function as tank destroyers

SPECIFICATIONS

Country of Origin: *Germany*

Crew: *4*

Weight: *21,600kg (47,628lb)*

Dimensions: *Length 5.38m (17ft 9in); width 2.92m (9ft 6in); height: 1.95m (6ft 5in)*

Range: *160km (99.4 miles)*

Armour: *16–80mm (0.62–3.14in)*

Armament: *One 75mm (2.95in) Stuk40 L/48 gun;*

Powerplant: *One Maybach HL120TR engine developing 221 kW (296 hp)*

Performance: *Maximum road speed 40km/h (25mph)*

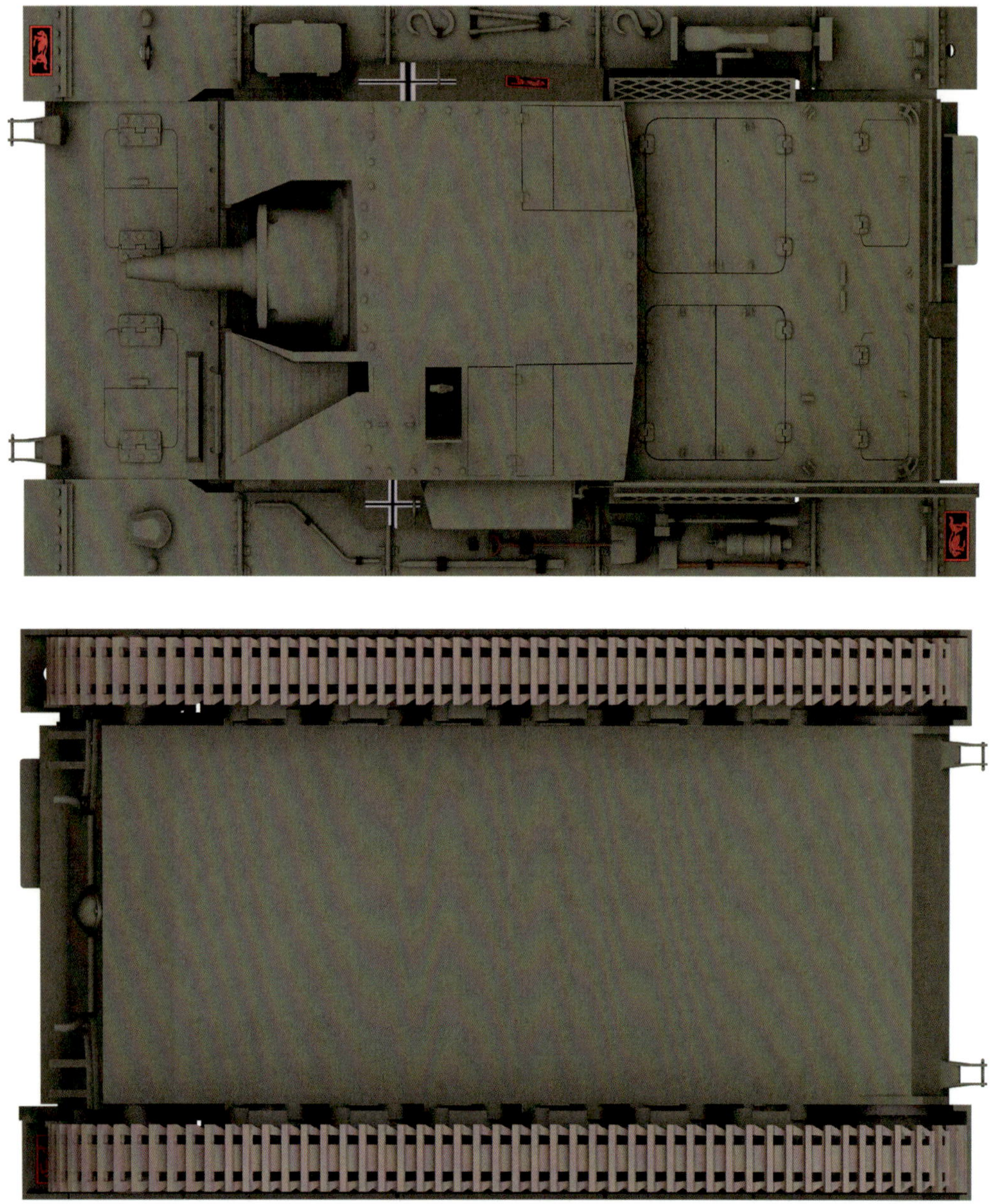

STuG III

The low silhouette of an assault gun made it a difficult target, and its armour was as good as that of the tank on which it was based. Used properly, it was an excellent support weapon.

SERIES OF UPGRADES

The STuG III was constantly updated as the war went on, with vehicles sent back for repair refitted to the standards of later models. Often, whatever parts were available were used, creating a vast range of sub-models built from components taken from several different variants. The most important change to the basic design was the longer gun, which marked a shift in the STuG III's role from an infantry support weapon to a general-purpose assault gun/tank destroyer. The longer gun increased anti-armour performance but could be an encumbrance when operating in urban terrain. From 1943 onwards, armoured side skirts were fitted to reduce vulnerability to shaped-charge infantry anti-armour weapons. The plates were often lost or damaged in the field, and were not always replaced.

Marder III

The German army made vast use of Czech-built PzKfpw 38(t) tanks, which were in many ways similar to the Panzer III and could be substituted for it. However, these tanks became obsolescent and a way had to be found to make use of them. Mounting captured Russian 76mm (3in) anti-tank guns on the chassis of a PzKpfw 38(t) created an improvised but effective Jadgpanzer (tank-hunter, or tank-destroyer). The vehicle was designated Marder II, and a version with a German 75mm (2.95in) gun was also built. However, the Marder II had a high silhouette, making it an easy target. A revised version, designated Marder III, was thus put into production. The Marder III's engine was moved forward and the gun housing positioned at the rear. The Marder III was simple and quick to manufacture, and did not absorb vast resources. Lightly armoured, it relied on concealment for survival. It was vulnerable to overhead shell bursts due to an open-topped fighting compartment. Although supplanted by more heavily-armoured vehicles, the Marder III was an effective combat asset and remained on the front lines until the end of the war.

- Tank destroyer with a crew of five
- 76.2mm (3in) anti-tank gun in open-topped mount
- Light armour and high silhouette

SPECIFICATIONS

Country of Origin: *Germany*

Crew: *4*

Weight: *10500kg (231,48lb)*

Dimensions: *Length 5.25m (17ft 2in); width 2.15m (7ft); height 2.48m (8ft 1in)*

Range: *190km (118 miles)*

Armour: *8–15mm (.3–59in)*

Armament: *One x 76.2mm (3in) Pak 40/3 L/46 gun: one 7.92mm).31in) MG34 machine gun*

Powerplant: *Praga AC gasoline 112kW (150hp)*

Performance: *Maximum road speed 42km/h (26mph)*

402

402

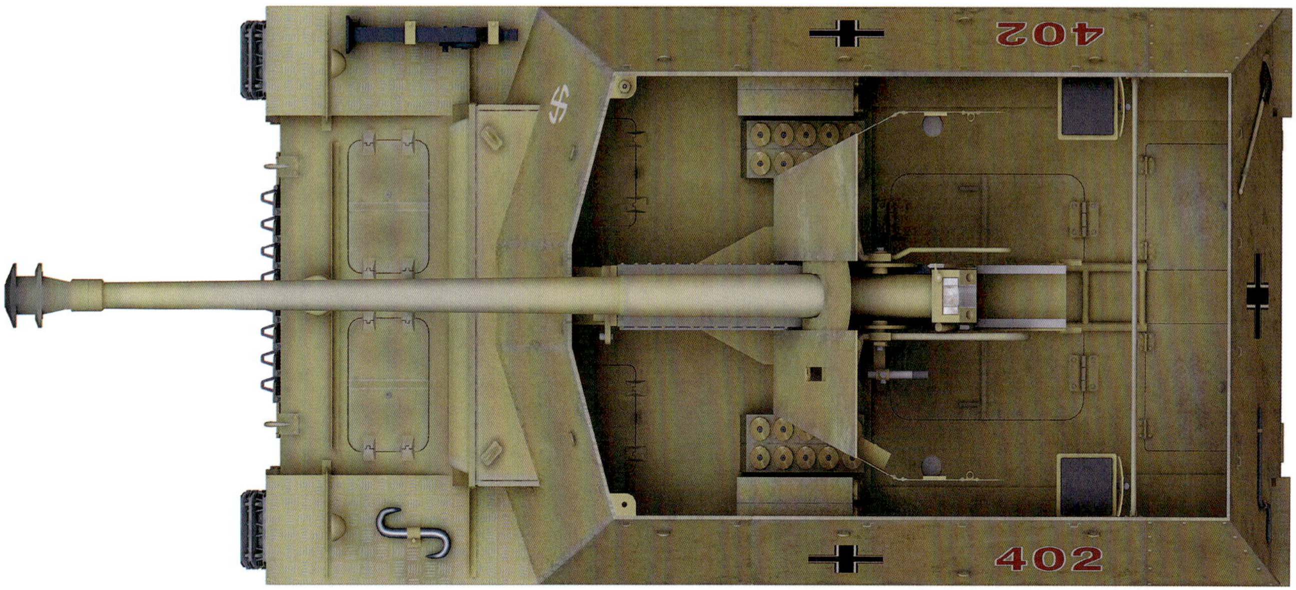
402
402

Marder III
The Marder III was vulnerable to artillery and even close-range machine gun fire, but could disable most Allied tanks at combat ranges. It was far more mobile than towed anti-tank guns and could quickly redeploy to deal with a new threat.

LIMITED EFFICIENCY

The use of a limited-traverse mount for the Marder's gun made construction much simpler and absorbed less resources than a turreted vehicle. The gun was capable of traversing 21° to either side, which allowed the engagement of several targets within the frontal arc without repositioning the vehicle. However, a Marder attacked from the flank would have to swivel the whole chassis to return fire, limiting its capabilities in a mobile action. The Marder III was thus a vehicle that did well when the odds were stacked in its favour, ideally firing from concealment into the flanks of enemy vehicles, but it suffered badly in a fair fight. Despite its limitations, the Marder III proved effective in action, and was produced in large numbers up until May 1944.

Semovente 75/18

Inspired by German assault guns, the Italian army decided to build some of its own. An existing chassis was fitted with a gun originally constructed for use in a towed configuration. The M13/40 medium tank was initially used as a basis, though later models were built on the M14/41 chassis instead. It was thought that the Semovente 75/18 would serve in a relatively distant fire support role, under divisional command. However, the vehicle was constructed with all-round armour protection, which proved good enough to enable deployment on the front lines. Thus the Semovente 75/18 served in both the self-propelled artillery and tank destroyer roles. It was armed with a short-barrelled 75mm (2.95in) weapon. Although its range was limited, the gun proved effective in action and could disable Allied M3 and M4 tanks with high-explosive anti-tank rounds. It could also fire high explosive and armour-piercing ammunition. Its main deficiency was the limited ammunition supply and small crew, which reduced rate of fire. Ammunition supply vehicles were eventually provided, which partially rectified this problem but could do nothing about the rate of fire.

- Self-propelled gun with a crew of three
- Armed with a short 75mm (2.95in) gun
- Fully enclosed, unlike many self-propelled artillery systems

SPECIFICATIONS

Country of Origin: *Italy*

Crew: *3*

Weight: *14,400kg (31,746lb)*

Dimensions: *Length 5.04m (16ft 6in); width 2.23m (7ft 4in); height: 1.85m (6ft 1in)*

Range: *230km (143 miles)*

Armour: *50mm (1.96in) (front)*

Armament: *One 75mm (2.95in) gun; one 8mm (.31in) machine gun*

Powerplant: *One SPA 15-TM-41 V-8 petrol engine developing 108kW (145hp)*

Performance: *Maximum road speed 38km/h (24mph)*

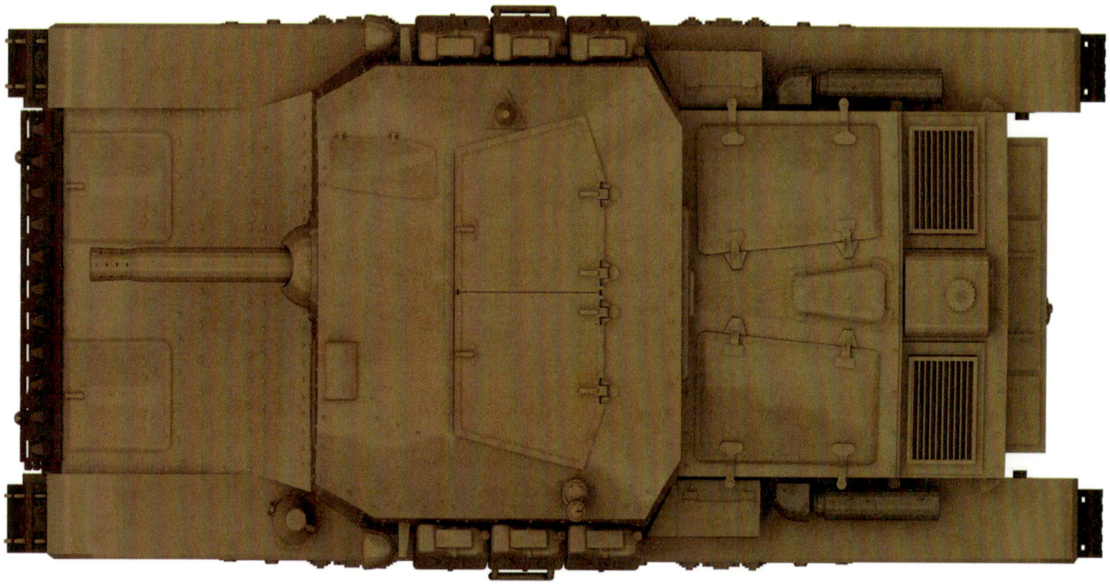

Semovente 75/18

The Semovente 75/18 was an artillery system, but it was more capable against enemy armour than Italian tanks. As a result it was often pushed into the front lines and forced to undertake operations better suited to real tanks.

A SUBSTITUTE TANK

The Semovente 75/18 was inspired by the highly successful German STuG III. Like many such vehicles, it was built on a tank chassis and mounted an already existing gun. In this case, the main armament had started out as a mountain gun but proved effective as an anti-tank weapon. A top-mounted machine gun was also carried for self-defence. However, there was no co-axial machine gun, which was a limitation when operating in a pseudo-tank role. The deployment of these vehicles was innovative, grouping them under divisional command rather than dispersing them lower down the chain of command. However, Italian tank design was generally poor, producing a series of flawed and ineffective vehicles that were no match for their British and American-made opponents. As a result, the Semovente 75/18 was often used as a substitute tank.

M7 Priest

The M7 Howitzer Motor Carriage used the chassis of the M3 medium tank, mated to a 105mm (4.1in) howitzer. The original design had limited ammunition capacity, just 24 rounds. Early in the production run this was increased to 69, with much of the ammunition stored under floor plates and 12 ready rounds along the outer walls of the fighting compartment. Gradual changes in the design resulted in later M7s using more components from the M4 Sherman tank than the original M3. The M7's armament was powerful but lacked range since it could not be elevated past 35°. This was due to insufficient room inside the vehicle, a requirement to keep the silhouette as low as possible. Post-war modifications increased the gun elevation to 65°. The M7 was deployed in large numbers by both US and British forces. British personnel thought the prominent cupola resembled a church pulpit and nicknamed the vehicle 'Priest', a designation later made official. The Priest was phased out of British service after the Sexton began to appear. Many M7s were converted into armoured personnel carriers nicknamed 'Kangaroos'.

- Self-propelled gun with a crew of seven
- Armed with a 105mm (4.1in) howitzer
- Deployed in huge numbers

SPECIFICATIONS

Country of Origin: *USA*

Crew: *7*

Dimensions: *Length 6.02m (19ft 9in); width 2.88m (9ft 5.25in); height 2.54m (8ft 4in)*

Range: *201km (125 miles)*

Armour: *Up to 25.4mm (1in)*

Armament: *One 105mm (4.1in) howitzer; one 12.7mm (0.5in) machine gun*

Powerplant: *One Continental nine-cylinder radial piston engine developing 279.6kW (375hp)*

Performance: *Maximum road speed 41.8km/h (26mph); fording 1.219m (4ft); vertical obstacle 0.61m (2ft); trench 1.91m (6ft 3in)*

US 3553524

US 3553524

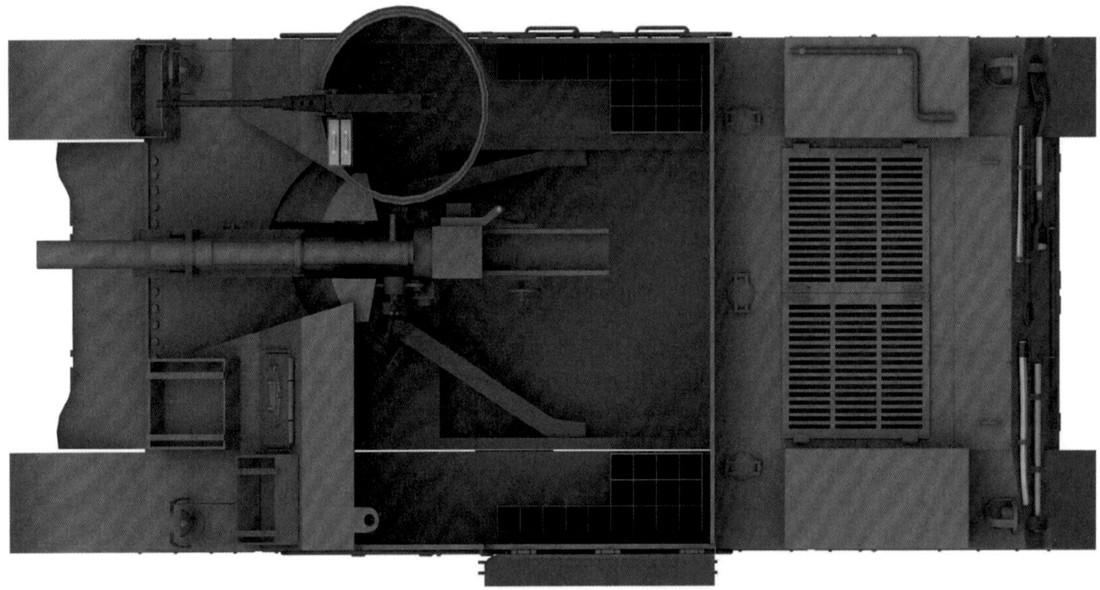

M7 Priest

The M7 Priest was sufficiently impressive that the British ordered 5500 of them. As artillery pieces they served in North Africa and Italy, and were also used for the invasion of Normandy, many continuing afterwards as personnel carriers.

DEEPCUT

MOBILE WARFARE

The M7 was not an assault gun but a self-propelled artillery piece. Of course, its main gun could be used for direct fire but its intended role was indirect artillery support. Built on an M3 tank chassis, the M7 was as mobile as the armoured forces it was created to support, enabling it to keep pace with a rapid advance or counter-attack. The cupola-mounted machine gun was a general-purpose weapon that could be used for air defence or to protect the vehicle from infantry attack. Ideally, artillery should not come into contact with enemy infantry, but there are never any guarantees in mobile warfare. Self-propelled artillery supporting an attack might penetrate quite deeply into enemy-held territory, and might find itself in the path of a counter-attack or encounter pockets of resistance.

Elefant

Tank destroyers mount an anti-tank gun in a fixed or limited-traverse mount. This has its limitations; a tank destroyer cannot traverse its weapon to engage a target to the side, and often cannot use a 'hull-down' protected position as a tank can. However, the lower silhouette makes the tank destroyer a more difficult target. Additionally, tank destroyers are cheaper and easier to manufacture than a tank mounting the same calibre of weapon. They are often built on an obsolete tank chassis, enabling older equipment to remain useful. The chassis for the Elefant heavy tank destroyer was the one put forward by Porsche for the Panzer VI Tiger project. The Porsche chassis was heavily protected and suitable as the basis for a heavily armoured vehicle mounting an 88mm (3.5in) anti-tank gun. The chassis received additional armour, with the gun carried in a fixed box superstructure. Some 90 Elefants were available for the Kursk offensive in 1943, but they suffered mechanical problems. The Elefant had no secondary weapon for infantry defence, so many were lost to infantry attacks in the close-quarters fighting around Kursk.

- Heavy tank destroyer with a crew of six
- 88mm (3.5in) anti-tank gun in limited-traverse mounting
- Secondary machine gun added after heavy losses to infantry attack

SPECIFICATIONS

Country of Origin: *Germany*

Creew: *6*

Dimensions: *Length 8.128m (26ft 8in); width 3.378m (11ft 1in); height 2.997m (9ft 10in)*

Range: *153km (95 miles)*

Armour: *50–200mm (1.97–7.87in)*

Armament: *One 88mm (3.5in) Pak 43/2 gun*

Powerplanet: *Two Maybach HL 120 TRM V-12 petrol engines each developing 395.2kW (530hp)*

Performance: *Maximum road speed 20.1km/h (12.5mph); fording 1m (3ft 4in); vertical obstacle 0.8m (31.5in); trench 2.65m (8ft 8.3in)*

524

524

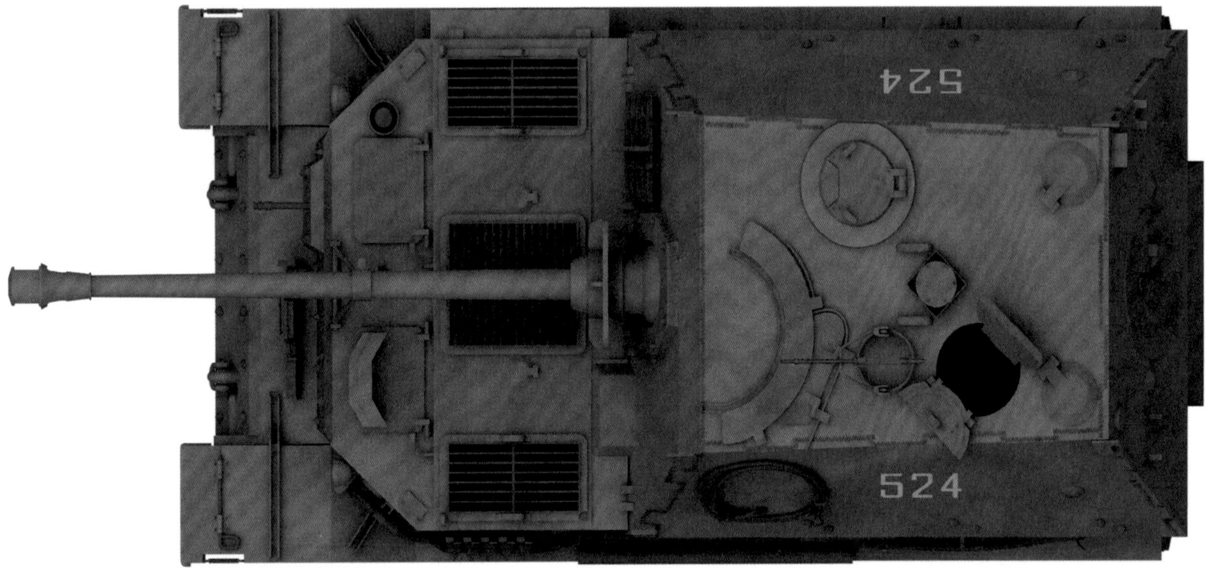
524
524

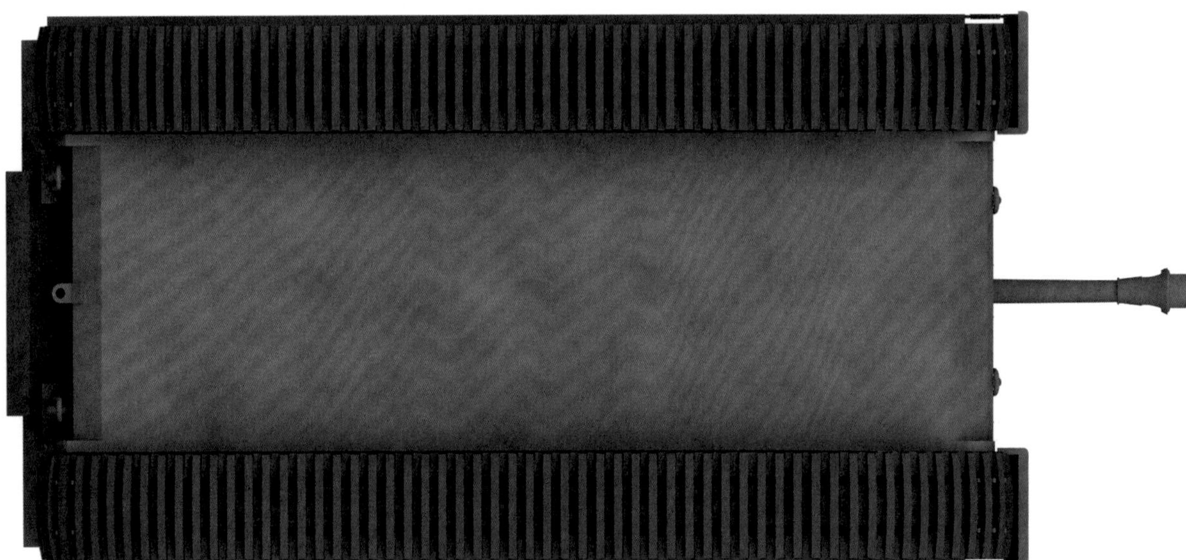

Elefant

The Elefant, also known as Ferdinand, should have been a potent force on the battlefield. It offered a means to get powerful and well protected anti-tank capability into action for a much lower cost than a Tiger tank.

HEAVY LOSSES

Like other heavy tanks and derived systems, the Elefant suffered from low speed and a limited radius of action. It was best suited to a defensive deployment, firing from ambush as enemy armour advanced. It originally had no secondary armament, which resulted in heavy losses at the Battle of Kursk. In the confused and highly mobile fighting, many enemy positions were bypassed by attacking units. This exposed support elements such as tank-destroyers to attack by enemy infantry, against whom the Elefant had no means of defence. Those Elefants that survived the battle, or which were recovered and repaired, were given a machine gun for infantry defence, but there were too few left for large-scale deployment. The remaining Elefants were used on an ad-hoc basis for the rest of the war.

Jagdtiger

The Jagdtiger was a tank destroyer based on the King Tiger (Tiger II) chassis. It was a massively armoured mobile emplacement rather than a true combat vehicle. Like many similar vehicles, the Jagdtiger had a high silhouette, making it a relatively easy target. However, there were few weapons that could penetrate its armour. The Jagdtiger carried the heaviest gun of any combat vehicle in the war, a 128mm (5in) weapon developed for the Maus supertank. Not enough of these guns were available, so some Jagdtigers were outfitted with 88mm (3.5in) guns instead. The limited traverse of the main armament was a drawback; the whole vehicle had to be turned in order to aim the gun, and this caused frequent transmission breakdowns. Some 150 Jagdtigers were initially ordered, but resources for their production were diverted, probably rightly, to the Panther tank production lines. Only 77 were completed, arriving in time to see combat during the defence of Hungary and to take part in the Ardennes offensive. The survivors were deployed piecemeal during the final Allied advance towards and into Germany.

- Tank destroyer with a crew of six
- Most Jagdtigers mounted a 128mm (5in) gun
- Anti-personnel grenade discharger fitted for close-in anti-infantry defence

SPECIFICATIONS

Country or Origin: *Germany*

Crew: *6*

Weight: *71,667kg (158,000lb)*

Dimensions: *Length 10.65m (34ft 11in); width 3.63m (11ft 11in); height 2.95m (9ft 8in)*

Range: *120km (75 miles)*

Armour: *250mm (9.84in)*

Armament: *One 128mm (5in) Pak 44 L/55 gun*

Powerplant: *One Maybach HL230P30 V-12 petrol engine developing 522kW (700hp)*

Performance: *Maximum road speed 38km/h (24mph)*

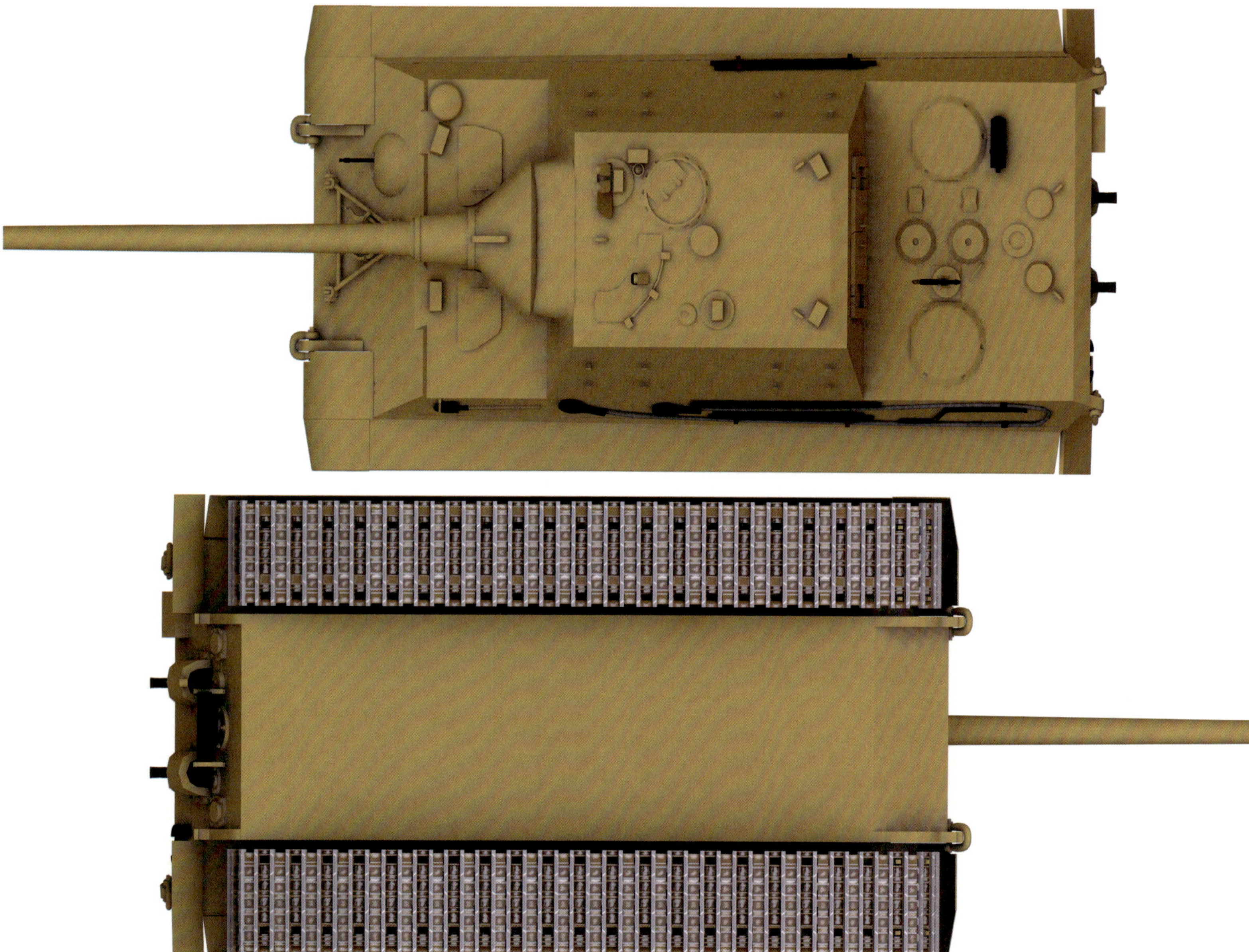

Jagdtiger

The Jagdtiger carried 38 to 40 rounds for its main gun. Shells were in two parts (projectile and propellant) and were handled by two loaders. Armour-piercing ammunition could destroy any Allied tank at ranges of 2000m (6562ft) or more.

HUNGRY FOR FUEL

The Jagdtiger made use of chassis and running gear developed by rival firms Henschel and Porsche for the King Tiger project. Most Jagdtigers were fitted with Henschel running gear, but 11 were completed with gear supplied by Porsche. The Jagdtiger suffered from very high fuel consumption at a time when fuel was in very short supply, and too few were available to create formal units. Instead, detachments were formed with the intention of assigning them wherever they could be most useful. Jagdtiger detachments took part in the Ardennes Offensive in 1944 but were limited by fuel availability. Afterwards, most ended their career as more or less static gun emplacements or were destroyed by their own crews after suffering breakdowns that could not be rectified in the field.

X7

ISU-122

Inspired by German assault guns, Soviet designers began to experiment with similar vehicles. The SU-122 entered production at the end of 1942. Mounting a 122mm (4.8in) gun on a T-34 chassis, some were available to fight in defence of Leningrad in January 1943. The SU-122 was found to be a highly effective tank destroyer, but was supplanted by the ISU-122, which entered production in the summer of 1943 and reached the front lines in early 1944. The new assault gun used the IS-2 chassis, but was otherwise similar to its predecessor. The ISU-122 was primarily intended for use as a heavy tank destroyer and performed well in this role. It was also an effective assault gun despite the length of its weapon, which made manoeuvring in urban terrain difficult. A variant designated ISU-122S was developed towards the end of the war, with a slightly improved gun giving increased armour penetration. It was expected that German armoured vehicles would continue the trend of the Panther and Tiger, becoming even more heavily armoured, but no new generation of tanks appeared for the enhanced ISU-122 to fight.

- Assault gun with a crew of five
- Armed with 122mm (4.8in) gun
- Built on IS-2 heavy tank chassis

SPECIFICATIONS

Country of Origin: *Soviet Union*

Crew: *5*

Weight: *45,500kg (100,372lb)*

Dimensions: *Length 9.85m (32ft 3in); width 3.07m (10ft 1in); height 2.48m (8ft 1in)*

Range: *220km (136.7 miles) (road)*

Armour: *90mm (3.54in) front*

Armament: *One 122mm (4.8in) A-19S gun; one 12.7mm (0.5in) DShk HMG*

Powerplant: *One V-2 diesel engine developing 447kW (600hp)*

Performance: *Maximum road speed 37km/h (23mph)*

ISU-122

The ISU-122 was almost identical to the ISU-152 self-propelled gun, other than systems connected with the weapon and its mountings. The IS-2 tank chassis proved an excellent basis for such systems, with ISU-122s remaining in service long after the end of the war.

A POWERFUL THREAT

The original SU-122 was built on a T-34 chassis. It distinguished itself in the bitter fighting around Leningrad early in 1943, proving very effective against enemy tanks. Some 1100 had been constructed by the middle of 1944, when the SU-122 was phased out in favour of the ISU-122, which used a heavy tank chassis but retained the same well-respected 122mm (4.8in) gun. The ISU-122 took part in the massive Bagration offensives of 1944 and the final drive into Germany. It could be used as a mobile artillery piece at need, but was more commonly deployed in the assault gun role. Although manoeuvring in urban terrain was something of a challenge due to the long gun, the ISU-122 was well regarded for its ability to blast enemy troops out of their positions with heavy direct fire.

M3 Halftrack

Halftrack vehicles offered some of the offroad capabilities of tracked vehicles, but far more cheaply and without the mechanical difficulties inherent in steering a fully-tracked vehicle. The US Army made extensive use of the M3 halftrack personnel carrier, which was based on a scout car design. A similar vehicle, the M2, was deployed as an artillery tractor. This had a rail around the top of the open rear compartment, allowing a machine gun to be mounted for all-round fire. The M3 did not have this feature, as it needed rear doors for personnel access. Over 40,000 M3 and M2 vehicles were used by the United States during the war, typically carrying 10 soldiers in addition to the three-man crew. Some vehicles were used to carry radios or other equipment and many carried supplies instead of troops. The M3A2 version increased its capacity to 12 personnel thanks to an improved internal layout, and also took over the artillery tractor role from the M2. Other variants included a conversion to carry an anti-tank gun or light artillery piece. These vehicles were not successful in action; the air-defence version was more effective.

- Lightly armoured personnel carrier with a crew of three
- Armed with a machine gun for self-defence
- Versions were built to carry anti-tank and anti-aircraft weapons

SPECIFICATIONS

Country of Origin: *USA*

Crew: *3*

Weight: *9299kg (20,458lb)*

Dimensions: *Length 6.18m (20ft 3.5in); width 2.22m (7ft 3.5in); height 2.26m (7ft 5in)*

Range: *282km (175 miles)*

Armour: *8mm (0.31in)*

Armament: *One 12.7mm (0.5in) machine gun; one 7.62mm (0.3in) machine gun*

Powerplant: *One White 160AX six-cylinder petrol engine developing 109.6kW (147hp)*

Performance: *Maximum road speed 64.4km/h (40mph); fording 0.81m (2ft 8in)*

U.S.A.
242724S

U.S.A.
242724S

M3 Halftrack
Early model M3s carried an unditching roller on the front bumper, to assist the vehicle in climbing out of an unexpectedly deep trench or hole. This was later replaced with a winch.

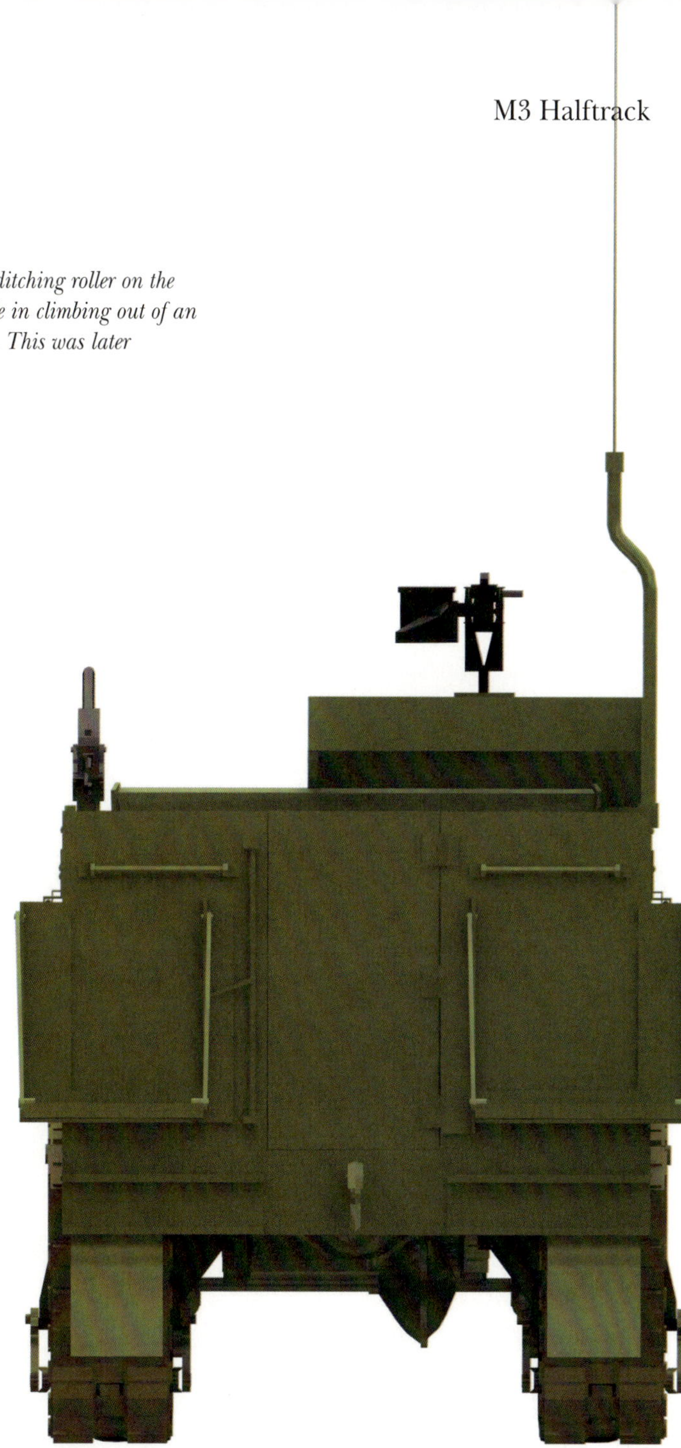

CHEAP AND EFFICIENT

Germany and the United States were the main wartime users of half-tracked vehicles, which were originally developed in France. Using the front wheels to steer and the tracks to provide rough-ground traction and mobility, the half-tracked truck was a cheap alternative to full-tracked personnel carriers and possessed better off-road performance than conventional trucks. It was thus well suited to keeping up with armoured forces, and was used to transport infantry as well as supplies and ammunition. Specialist versions mounting various weapons were also created, of which the anti-aircraft variant was by far the most successful. Some 3400 AA vehicles were built on the M3 chassis or one of its many variants. However, despite the usefulness of these vehicles, they fell out of use after the war.

RUE
DU CLOITRE
NOTRE-DAME
49850

LVT-1

The Landing Vehicle Tracked (LVT) concept was demonstrated in the 1930s by a vehicle known as the 'Alligator', for use in the Florida Everglades. Capable of driving itself through water by using its tracks as paddles, the Alligator had good off-road mobility on dry (or swampy) land. This was exactly what the US Marine Corps needed to support its amphibious operations, and a developed version designated LVT-1 was bought. The 'Amphibious Tractor' became known as Amtracks. They were intended for use as transports and logistics vehicles rather than in the assault role, and were not well armed or protected. Amtracks proved extremely useful despite their shortcomings, and by 1944 a new model designated LVT (A)1 was entering service. This was a specially designed assault vehicle, with good armour protection for the crew and up to 24 Marines in the rear compartment. Armed with a 37mm (1.45in) gun and a machine gun, the new Amtrack could convey its troops onto the beach and give fire support when it got there. A series of improved variants on the LVT concept followed the LVT-1, culminating in the LVT-4.

- Amphibious assault vehicle with a crew of three
- Capable of transporting up to 24 Marines
- Initially unprotected; later versions were well armoured

SPECIFICATIONS

Country of Origin: *USA*

Crew: *3*

Weight: *10,800kg (23,760lb)*

Dimensions: *Length 7.95m (26ft 1in); width 3.25m (10ft 8in); height 3.023m (9ft 11in)*

Range: *Road radius 241km (150 miles); water radius 120.7km (75 miles)*

Armour: *Up to 67mm (2.63in)*

Armament: *One 37mm (1.45in) cannon (later 75mm/2.95in howitzer); one 7.62mm (0.3in) machine gun*

Powerplant: *Two Cadillac petrol engines developing a total of 164.1kW (220hp)*

Performance: *Maximum land speed 27.3km/h (17mph); maximum water speed 9.7km/h (6mph); fording amphibious*

A 16
US NAVY

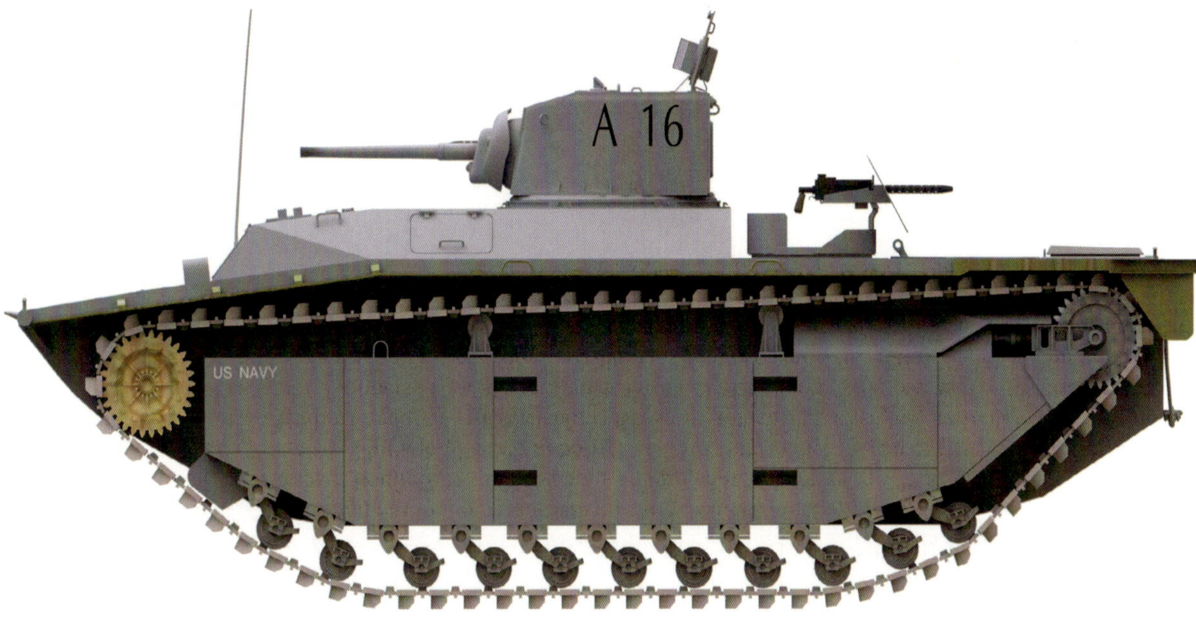
A 16
US NAVY

LVT-1

The most dangerous part of any amphibious operation was crossing the open beach under fire. The LVT series of vehicles provided a means to get troops safely across the killing zone and into cover.

A RANGE OF USES

Initially conceived as a transport vehicle, the Amtrack was envisaged as supporting amphibious operations by bringing supplies ashore. However, it soon became an essential part of Marine amphibious operations. Armoured versions soon followed, expanding into a range of roles, including personnel transport and fire support. Although a somewhat clumsy vehicle on land, the Amtrack had the advantage that it could get itself ashore rather than needing landing craft or a port, so was often used in preference to vehicles that might have performed better once ashore but which were unable to reach land unassisted. Conversions to the air defence, heavy weapons platform and engineering tractor roles enabled the LVT to establish itself as indispensable. Modern Marine forces use a vehicle which, while more sophisticated, is broadly the same in function.

SdKfz 250

The SdKfz 250 was a small personnel carrier that could also act as a supply vehicle but was adapted for various roles. Unofficial conversions included air-defence vehicles improvised in the field, and reconnaissance or artillery observation, as well as all-terrain transport for officers. The standard model carried four troops plus the crew of two, and mounted a machine gun in a shield at the front of the open rear compartment. A mounting for the carried infantry's own support weapon was positioned at the rear. The main flaw of the SdKfz 250 was a poor interior layout, which made it difficult to use the available space: the radio sets filled much of the interior, and command vehicles suffered from a lack of working space for the officers using them. Successful SdKfz 250 variants included observation and communications vehicles and light reconnaissance models. The latter were equipped with a turret mounting a 20mm (0.79in) cannon. Tank destroyer versions and fire support vehicles, equipped with guns of up to 75mm (2.95in), were also produced in numbers.

- Small personnel carrier with a crew of two
- Armed with a general-purpose machine gun
- Small and cramped, with inadequate internal space

SPECIFICATIONS

Country of Origin: *Germany*

Crew: *2*

Weight: *5340kg (11,775lb)*

Dimensions: *Length 4.56m (14ft 11.5in); width 1.95m (6ft 4.8in); height 1.66m (5ft 5.4in)*

Range: *350km (220 miles)*

Armour: *(Steel) 15mm (0.59in) maximum*

Armament: *One 7.92mm (0.31in) MG34 machine gun*

Powerplant: *One Maybach hL 42 6-cylinder diesel, developing 89kW (120hp) at 3000rpm*

Performance: *Maximum road speed 65km/h (40mph); fording 0.75m (2.46ft); gradient 24 per cent*

GREIF

GREIF

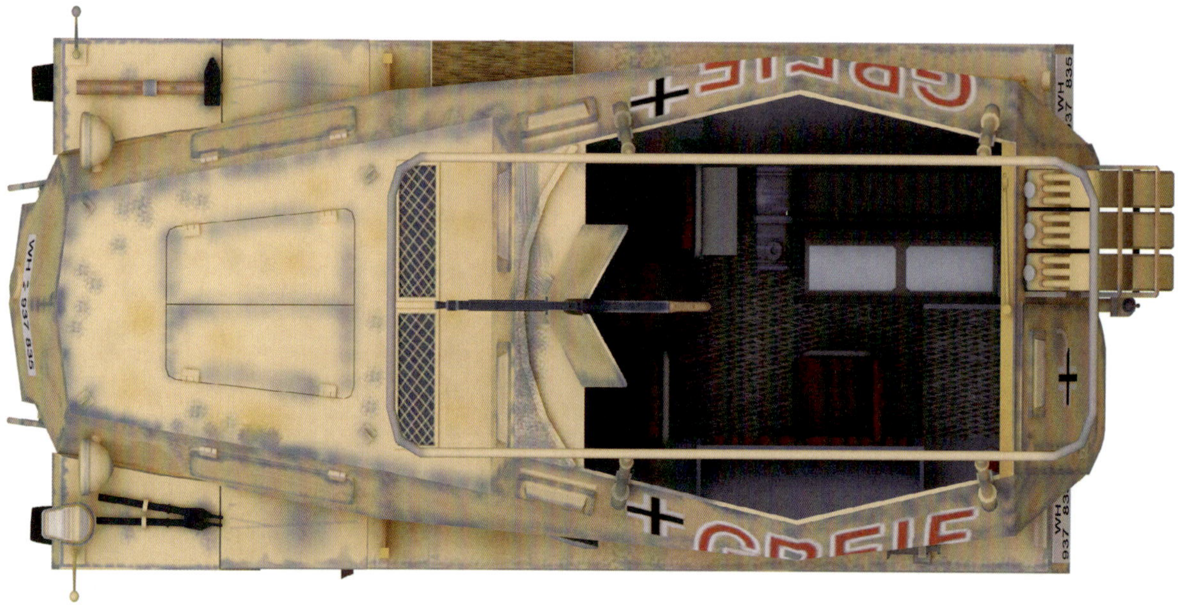

SdKfz 250

Although the SdKfz 250 was too small for its intended task, it was available at a time when there were few alternatives. The first examples entered service in 1940 and production continued until the end of the war.

THREAT OF GRENADES

The SdKfz 250 was used for a range of transport and utility purposes. It was suited to the reconnaissance and artillery observation role, but was less effective as a personnel transport because it could carry only half a squad of infantry. The armoured sides offered good protection against direct fire when in contact with the enemy, but the open top was a liability. Troops riding inside were vulnerable to fragmentation from bursting shells, and also enemy fire directed from above. Grenades were a severe threat, especially when operating in close terrain. The effect of a grenade thrown or dropped into an open-topped box from which the occupants could not quickly escape could be catastrophic. Vaulting over the sides was generally a quicker way to exit the vehicle than using the rear access door.

Kettenkraftrad

The Kettenkraftrad was a light transport and utility vehicle with twin tracks and a single wheel to steer. The driver had a car-type seat, and all steering functions were carried out by turning the handlebars. For shallow turns the front wheel would guide the vehicle, but a greater movement of the handlebars caused a track brake to be applied on the relevant side, increasing manoeuvrability in confined spaces. The Kettenkraftrad was designed to be air-mobile, and could be carried in the hold of a Ju52. Its main function with airmobile troops was as a gun tractor, though it could also carry supplies. In this role, a small trailer was used to increase the Kettenkraftrad's rather slight capacity. As a personnel transport it was of limited utility, since it could carry only two men in addition to the driver. The Kettenkraftrad served mainly in Russia and North Africa, where its tracks enabled it to deal with snow, mud and soft sand and to climb steep slopes. It was also used as an aircraft tractor. Production began in 1940, with active military service beginning in 1941 during Operation *Barbarossa*.

- Light half-tracked utility vehicle
- Not capable of mounting any weapons
- Used as a gun tractor and logistics vehicle

SPECIFICATIONS

Country of Origin: *Germany*

Crew: *1*

Weight: *1280kg (2822lb)*

Dimensions: *Length 3m (9ft 10in); width 1.2m (3ft 10in); height 1m (3.3ft)*

Range: *250km (150 miles)*

Armour: *None*

Armament: *None*

Powerplant: *One Opel Olympia 38 petrol, developing 27kW (36hp)*

Performance: *Maximum road speed: 80km/h (50mph)*

WH-371 209

WH-371 209

Kettenkraftrad

Passenger transport used two rather basic rear-facing seats, making travel over rough terrain something of an unpleasant experience for the troops riding the vehicle. Almost 9000 were built before production ceased in 1944, with more constructed for agricultural use after the end of the war.

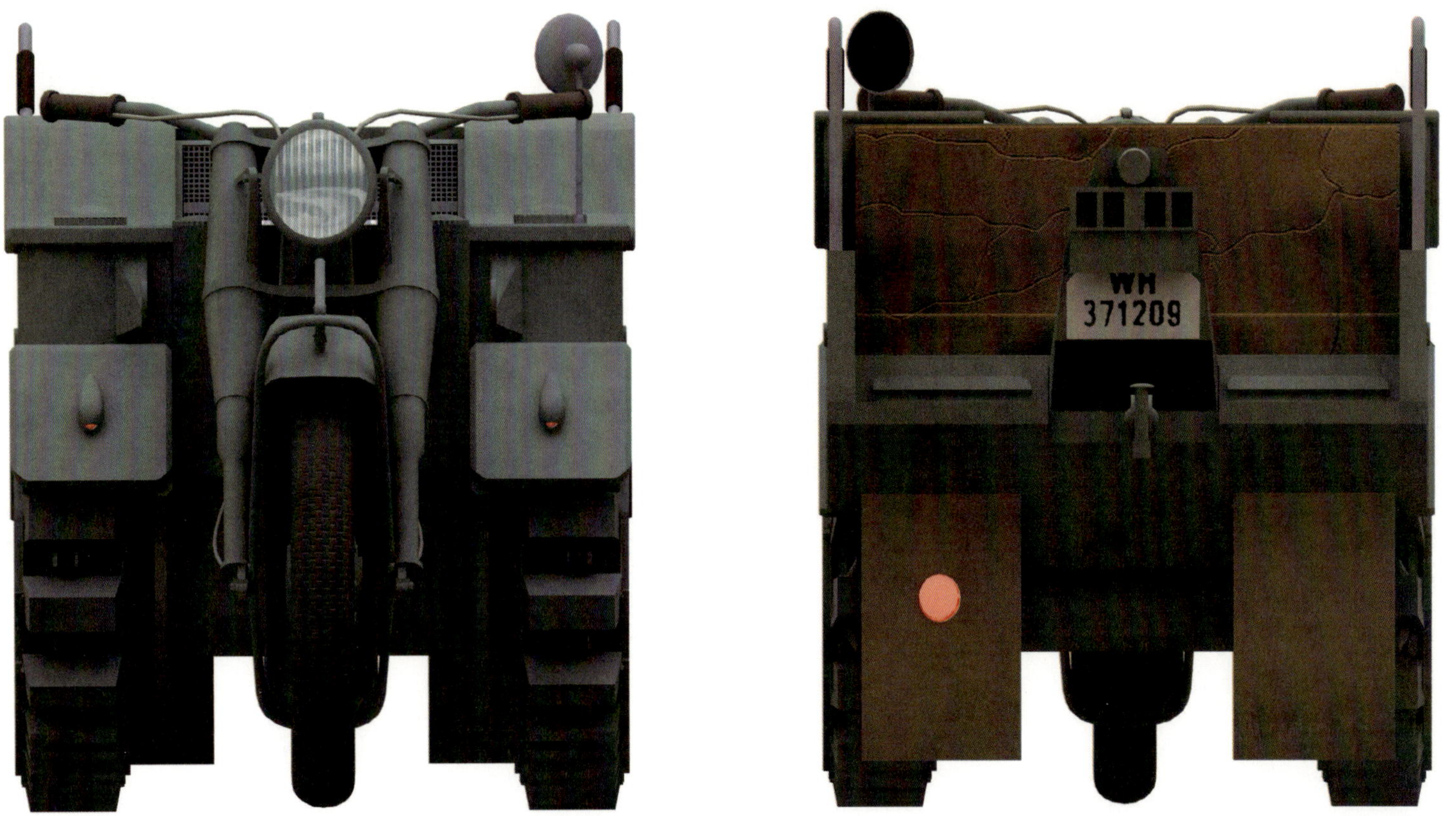

ON ROUGH GROUND

The Kettenkraftrad was an ungainly-looking vehicle, but one that offered certain significant advantages. It could cross terrain where a dispatch motorcycle would become hopelessly stuck, and could carry somewhat more. Under most circumstances, steering was accomplished by steering the front wheel like a motorcycle, but the tracks could be braked to provide extra turning capability at need. Mobility on rough ground and slope-climbing were both very good, though the Kettenkraftrad suffered from the same problem as some German tanks. In that its overlapping road wheels were prone to becoming clogged with mud, and in Russia this frequently froze solid and immobilized the vehicle. The Kettenkraftrad served as a general light-transport vehicle in most theatres of the war, including Western Europe, Russia and North Africa.

Schwimmwagen

The Allies considered their small utility vehicle, the Willys Jeep, to be one of their four 'war-winning tools'. For the Axis forces, the equivalent was the Volkswagen Kübelwagen. The Schwimmwagen was an amphibious variant on the basic Kübelwagen. To create a vehicle that was amphibious with no preparation – i.e. it could be driven straight into and across a body of water and out again – a new tublike hull form had to be developed rather than the flat-bottomed Kübelwagen. The original Type 128 model was watertight but structurally weak, leading to damage when driving offroad. A smaller but structurally more robust version, designated Type 166, was put into mass production with over 15,000 built by the end of the war. The Schwimmwagen was normally a two-wheel-drive vehicle, but could engage four-wheel-drive in first gear and on some models, in reverse. It was driven through water using a propeller that was lowered into position when needed. The vehicle could also move in water using the rotation of its wheels. This was necessary if reversing was desired; the propeller drive only worked in one direction.

- Light transport and utility vehicle
- Sometimes armed with a general-purpose machine gun
- Equipped with propeller drive in addition to wheels

SPECIFICATIONS

Country of Origin: *Germany*

Crew: *1*

Weight: *910kg (2007lb)*

Dimensions: *Length 3.82m (12ft 6in); width 1.48m (4ft 10in); height 1.61m (5ft 3in)*

Range: *520km (320 miles)*

Armour: *None*

Armament: *None*

Powerplant: *One VW 4-cylinder petrol engine, developing 19kW (25hp)*

Performance: *Maximum road speed 80km/h (50mph)*

Kfz: K 2s
Leergew.0,83t
Nutzlast.0,45t
VL. Kl. II

Kfz: K 2s

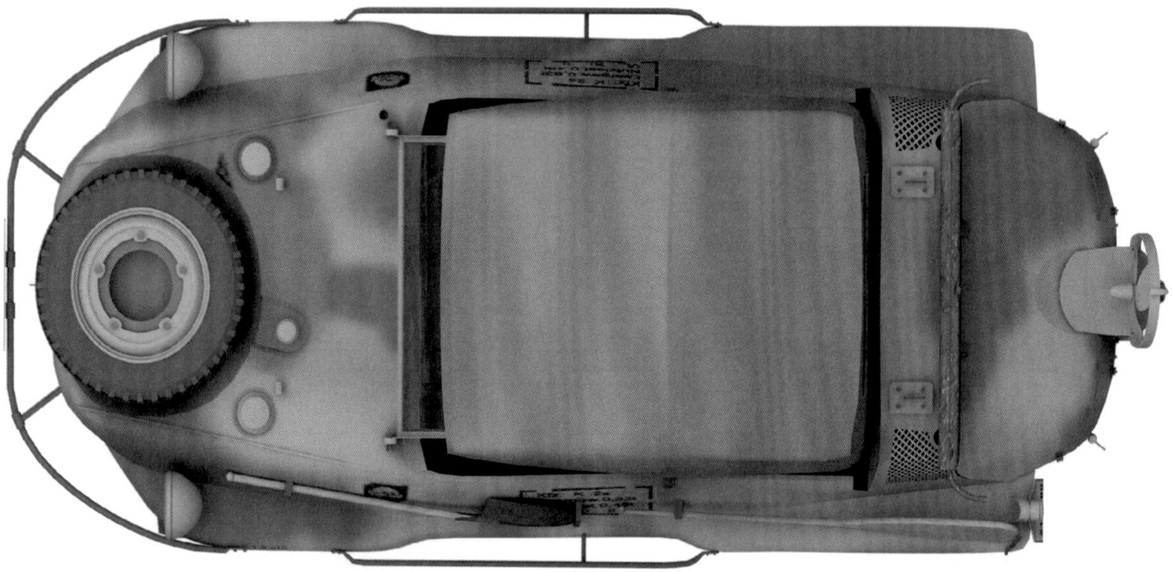

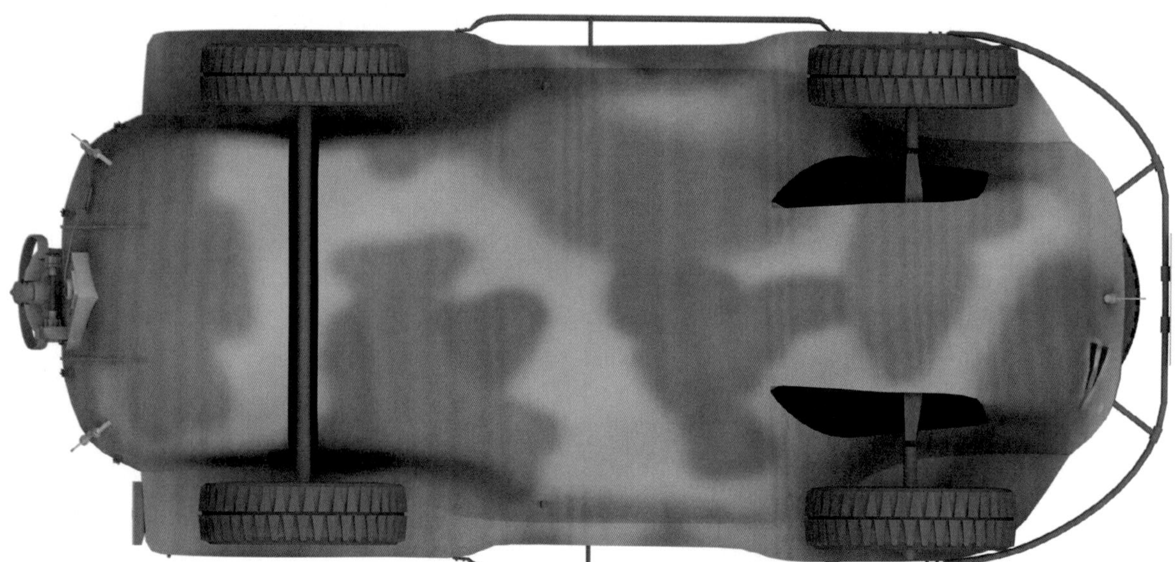

Schwimmwagen
Utility vehicles play an essential part in mobile warfare. They are needed in vast numbers as personnel transports, staff cars, mail trucks, liaison vehicles and ersatz reconnaissance platforms. The Schwimmwagen was robust and reliable, and capable of handling calm waters with ease. In the event of breakdown or tricky manoeuvring, oars were carried as standard.

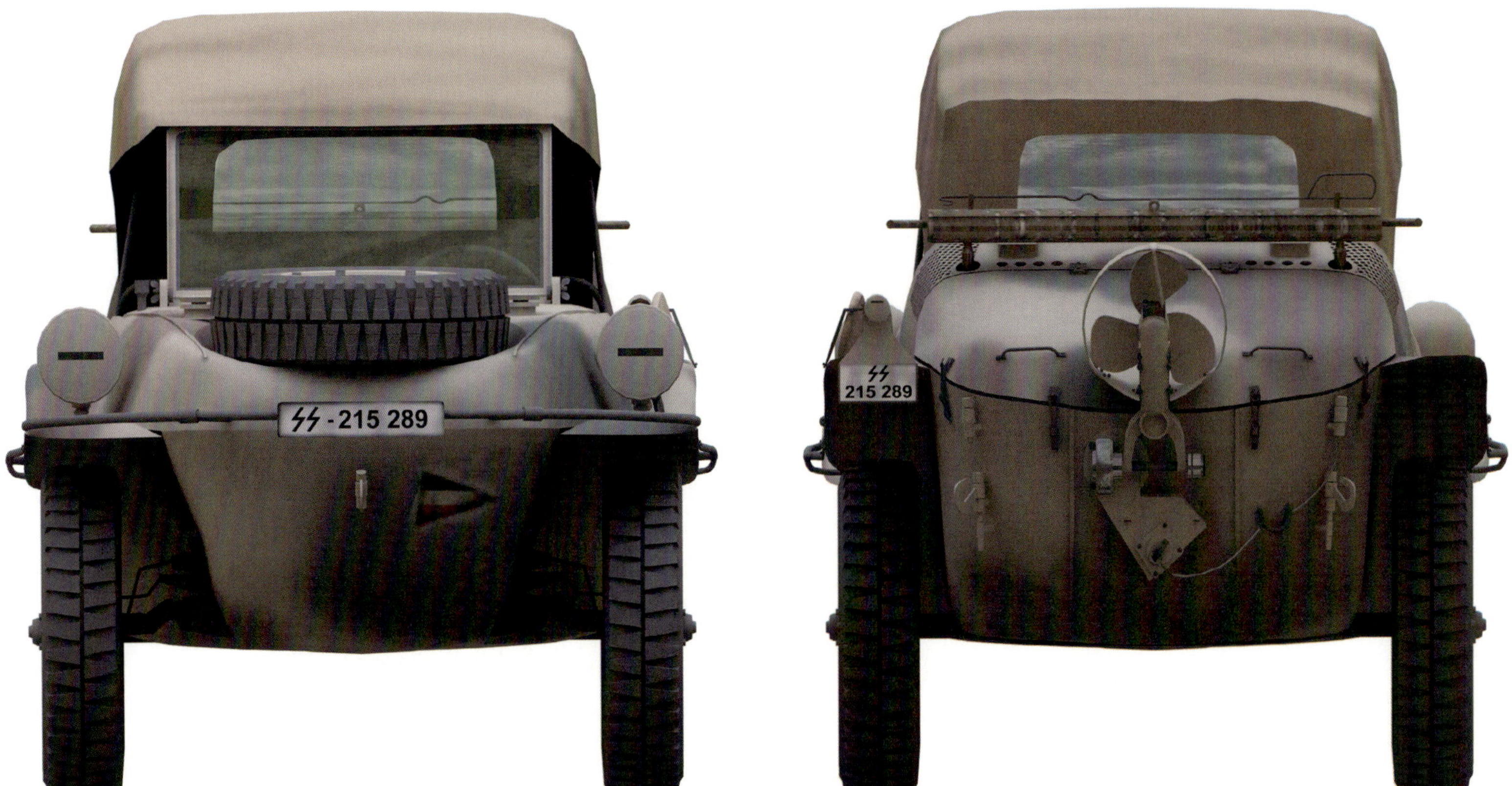

Glossary

amphibious Describing or related to forces landing from the sea.
chassis The frame on which the body of an automobile or tank is mounted.
co-axial Having a common axis.
encumbrance A burden or obstruction.
envisage To imagine or contemplate.
ersatz Synthetic or artificial.
fillet A raised rim on the muzzle of a gun.
howitzer A cannon with a short barrel used to fire projectiles at high trajectories.
hull The main body of a ship, tank, or other vessel.
impunity Exemption from punishment or consequences.
invulnerable Incapable of being wounded or damaged.
lathe To cut with a lathe, that is, a machine for shaping wood or metal via rotating tools.
pillbox An enclosed structure of reinforced concrete for machines guns, as part of a defensive position.
reconnaissance Military observation for strategic purposes, such as locating the enemy.
spurious False or fraudulent.
turret A rotating structure mounted to a tank from which guns can be mounted and fired.
winch A crank that is used to pull in or let out a cable or rope.

For More Information

Canadian War Museum
1 Vimy Place
Ottawa, ON K1A 0M8
Canada
(800) 555-5621
Website: http://www.warmuseum.ca
The Canadian War Museum showcases the military history of Canada, covering all branches of the Canadian armed forces in addition to the experience of citizens at home.

The National World War II Museum
945 Magazine St.
New Orleans, LA 70130
(504) 528-1944
Website: http://www.nationalwwiimuseum.org
The National World War II Museum includes multimedia exhibits, artifacts, and oral histories that tell the story of the United States' involvement in World War II from the front lines to the home front. Its website features extensive digital collections and virtual field trips.

The Imperial War Museum
Lambeth Rd.
London SE1 6HZ
United Kingdom
Website: http://www.iwm.org.uk
The Imperial War Museum, which has several locations across the United Kingdom, often exhibits World War II–era tanks. On its website, visitors can learn about World War II and other conflicts.

The Tank Museum
Linsay Rd.
Bovington, Dorset BH20 6JG
United Kingdom
+44 01929 462359
Website: http://www.tankmuseum.org
The Tank Museum traces the history of armored warfare from World War I to the present. Its exhibits include over three hundred vehicles, which are also profiled on the museum's websites.

World War II Veterans Committee
The American Veterans Center
1100 N. Glebe Rd., Suite 910
Arlington, VA 22201
(703) 302-1012
Website: http://www.americanveteranscenter.org/vet-committees/wwii-veterans
The World War II Veterans Committee shares the legacy of World War II for its veterans and future generations through publications, oral histories, and documentaries that record veterans' stories from the war.

Websites

Because of the changing nature of Internet links, Rosen Publishing has developed an online list of websites related to the subject of this book. This site is updated regularly. Please use this link to access the list:

http://www.rosenlinks.com/MT/Tank

For Further Reading

Barron, Leo. *Patton at the Battle of the Bulge: How the General's Tanks Turned the Tide at Bastogne.* New York, NY: NAL Caliber, 2014.

Bishop, Chris, ed. *The Illustrated Encyclopedia of Weapons of World War II.* London, England: Amber Books, 2014.

DiNicolo, Gina M. *The Black Panthers, a Story of Race, War, and Courage: The 761st Tank Battalion in World War II.* Yardley, PA: Westholme Publishing, 2014.

Elson, Aaron. *The Armored Fist: The 712th Tank Battalion in the Second World War.* Oxford, England: Fonthill Media, 2013.

Estes, Kenneth. *Super-Heavy Tanks of World War II.* Oxford, England: Osprey Publishing, 2014.

Gilbert, Oscar E. *Tanks in Hell: A Marine Corps Tank Company on Tarawa.* Haverford, PA: Casemate Publishers, 2015.

Haskew, Michael. *The World's Greatest Tanks: An Illustrated History.* London, England: Amber Books, 2014.

Hoth, Hermann. *Panzer Operations: Germany's Panzer Group 3 During the Invasion of Russia, 1941.* Haverford, PA: Casemate Publishers, 2015.

Milner, Mark. *Stopping the Panzers: The Untold Story of D-Day* (Modern War Studies). Lawrence, KS: University Press of Kansas, 2014.

Ogorkiewicz, Richard. *Tanks: 100 Years of Evolution* (General Military). Oxford, England: Osprey Publishing, 2014.

Porter, David. *Allied Tanks of World War II* (World's Great Weapons). London, England: Amber Books, 2014.

Zaloga, Steve. *Armored Champion: The Tanks of World War II.* Mechanicsburg, PA: Stackpole Books, 2015.

Index

Page references in *italics* refer to illustration captions

Picture Credits

All Artworks © Military Visualizations, Inc. (www.milviz.com)

Photographs:

Alamy: 64 (Interfoto)

Amber Books: 89

Art-Tech/Aerospace: 17, 59, 124, 178, 209

Art-Tech/MARS: 22/23, 52/53, 83, 155, 196/197

Cody Images: 28, 34/35, 40/41, 46/47, 58, 70/71, 76/77, 82, 88, 94/95, 100/101, 106/ 107, 112/113, 118, 130/131, 142, 148/149, 154, 160/161, 166, 167, 172/173, 179, 184/185, 191, 202/203, 208, 214, 215, 220, 221

Nick Cornish: 29, 65, 119, 125, 136, 143, 190

Mary Evans Picture Library: 16 (Robert Hunt Collection)

Topfoto: 137 (RIA Novosti)